U.S. Foreign Policy and Christian Ethics

BOOKS PUBLISHED BY THE WESTMINSTER PRESS

By John C. Bennett and Harvey Seifert

U.S. Foreign Policy and Christian Ethics

By John C. Bennett

The Radical Imperative:
From Theology to Social Ethics

By Harvey Seifert

New Power for the Church

Reality and Ecstasy:
A Religion for the 21st Century

Ethical Resources for Political
and Economic Decision

Power Where the Action Is

Conquest by Suffering: The Process and Prospects
of Nonviolent Resistance

*By Harvey Seifert
in collaboration with Howard J. Clinebell, Jr.*

Personal Growth and Social Change: A Guide for Ministers
and Laymen as Change Agents

U.S. FOREIGN POLICY AND CHRISTIAN ETHICS

by
JOHN C. BENNETT
and
HARVEY SEIFERT

THE WESTMINSTER PRESS
Philadelphia

Book Design by Dorothy Alden Smith

First edition

Published by The Westminster Press®
Philadelphia, Pennsylvania

PRINTED IN THE UNITED STATES OF AMERICA

9 8 7 6 5 4 3 2 1

Library of Congress Cataloging in Publication Data

Bennett, John Coleman, 1902–
    U.S. foreign policy and Christian ethics.

    Bibliography: p.
    1. International relations—Moral and religious aspects. 2. United States—Foreign relations—1945–   I. Seifert, Harvey, joint author.
II. Title.
JX1255.B45   261.8'7   77-5062
ISBN 0-664-24756-3

CONTENTS

PREFACE

THE IDEA of writing this book together grew out of a course that we gave in 1975 in the School of Theology at Claremont. We discovered that there is very little systematic writing on "U.S. Foreign Policy and Christian Ethics." Each of us had written a brief book on the subject more than ten years ago but these books are now out of date and out of print. There are many books from a Christian point of view on narrower problems of war and peace or international violence. Many Christians have written on such specific subjects as world poverty and the struggles for liberation in Latin America and elsewhere. These subjects are important for American foreign policy, but we felt that a more comprehensive and systematic book in the field was needed. We are grateful to our publishers for encouragement in this enterprise.

Those who know us sometimes think of us as having different backgrounds in theological ethics. We have found that we are in close agreement in our criticisms of existing structures and policies and in our views concerning the most needed modifications of American foreign policy and of the attitudes of the American people toward old tensions between East and West and toward the growing tensions between rich and poor nations in the world's North and South. We are also jointly concerned about new problems such as those connected with the global environment shared by all nations. We agree basically on the issues involved in the debates among Christians between pacifists and nonpacifists. Both of us have benefited from mutual criticism of all chapters, and our collaboration on Chapter 5, "Personal Options and Modern War," has been especially close.

There are differences of emphasis between us only on how close an approximation to Christian goals can be expected of nations even in the long run and in the precise weighing of positive and negative factors in Communist movements and regimes. We have not tried to achieve uniformity on such matters, and it is well for the reader to know that apart from our joint responsibility for Chapter 5, John Bennett takes full responsibility for Chapters 1, 3, 4, 7, and 8 and Harvey Seifert takes full responsibility for Chapters 2, 6, 9, 10, and 11.

One contribution of this book may be that it demonstrates the substantial agreement possible within the Christian community between persons who start with somewhat different theological assumptions. On those basic features of U.S. foreign policy on which the life of our nation and peace and justice in the world so largely depend, our faith provides a common perspective for criticism. We hope that our book may be of some help at a time when the emergence of new issues, concerning which positions are not yet fixed, is causing people to become much more open to change in their views of the relation of our country to other nations.

Something should be said about the title. This book is not a systematic examination of U.S. foreign policy. However, when we set out to deal with some of the issues raised by foreign policy in general, we realized that we were writing about them in the context of the foreign policy of our own country. For this reason we decided to refer to U.S. foreign policy in the title.

Readers have good reason to ask how specific political and economic judgments made in this book are related to Chrstian ethics. We do not think of them as having been deduced directly from Christian ethics. We could have chosen to discuss Christian motives, goals, and principles in a historical vacuum but we thought it would be more useful to provide an example of risking specific judgments in our situation as we try to be faithful to our understanding of Christian ethics. Sometimes negative judgments about the human consequences that are *known* of particular foreign policies can be derived from our theological and ethical convictions. Also, judgments concerning the presuppositions, the motives, and the goals that should control policies can be derived from those convictions. We are more concerned to suggest the direction of future policies than we are to suggest precise legislation, structures, or actions. Estimates concerning what is possible in a given situation depend upon what we have learned from specific forms of expertise and from our own observation of the facts of the situation, and we recognize that ethics is not the determining factor here. Also, sometimes these estimates involve risks. We often emphasize the dilemmas which all who make decisions about foreign policy confront. We do not intend to suggest that there is only one way of resolving such dilemmas consistent with Christian ethics. Yet we do suggest that some of the recommended ways of resolving them require a heavier burden of proof than others. Some should be rejected as incompatible not only with Christian ethics but also with the more broadly based humane ethics which is recognized to have authority in our pluralistic nation. We believe that it is a ground for hope that so much that we, as Christians, seek for our nation and the world is supported by the best vision of the just and humane society in our national tradition.

JOHN C. BENNETT
HARVEY SEIFERT

1

Theological and Ethical Presuppositions

THERE IS NO AREA of life in which humanity has a greater stake than international relations. Its very survival is involved. Yet it is an area of most acute difficulty for Christian ethics or for any humane and universal ethics. So deep and stubborn are the moral problems in international relations that many Christians have been content to declare that there is a double standard: one standard for personal life and for more limited social relations, and another for the national state, especially in its relations with other national states. We shall emphasize the problems that lead to such a conclusion. But at the outset we say that this book is based on the belief that, great as are the tensions between Christian ethics and international politics, the two should not be separated. All that Christians do, or to which they give consent, in this area of their lives should be kept under Christian judgment. The moral commitments and sensitivities inspired by their faith should be determining factors in their choice of national goals and in their motives as citizens. The acceptance of moral limits in the choice of means is crucial. It is true that politics is the art of the possible. But this maxim is misused when it is assumed that the possible is static and cannot be changed.

MORAL OBSTACLES IN INTERNATIONAL RELATIONS

Why are the problems of international relations often so morally recalcitrant? The answers to that question are written large in history and in contemporary events. We shall briefly illustrate some of them at many points in this book.

Moral relations between people in different nations are extremely thin and precarious. To be sure, they are not uniform around the world, and between some nations there are ties of common culture and of grateful memories that do support generally constructive mutual relationships. One illustration of this is the remarkable fact that even the American revolution against the British crown is now seen as a tie between Britain and the United States. But cultural differences, often involving a background of religious differences, and geographical distance seriously limit imagination and sympathy in human relations across national boundaries. Geographical proximity does not guarantee that conditions will be any better, as is evident in the relationship between close neighbors in the Middle East. Ideological conflicts, mutual fears that have a long history, and mutual hostility and vindictiveness that go back to particular wounds given and received often compound the effects of the general obstacles to friendly and trustful mutuality between nations. Conflicts of economic interest are often present. They are frequently seen as threatening a nation's survival or consigning it to a one-sided dependence on a more powerful neighbor. We need not take a fatalistic attitude toward these many causes of hostility. Who would have predicted a generation ago that there would be as good relations as exist today between Germany and France, or Japan and the United States?

A sense of basic insecurity, not least evident between the strongest powers, casts a dark shadow on international relations. Since no dependable collective security system exists, nations are driven to conclude that their security against attack or at least against blackmail, depends on their own power, especially military power. The dangers that threaten nations are fateful because of modern weapons. Because of the possibility of nuclear annihilation, even the strongest nations, because they arouse fear in others, feel insecure if they let down their guard. The whole world suffers from this mutual fear of the giants. The giants themselves are distorted in their own priorities by this fear. They prepare to destroy each other's populations in the hope that such preparations will prevent the war in which this annihilation might take place. In the meantime they cultivate callousness concerning the moral consequences of their actions if war should come.

There is a persistent moral and psychological problem within each nation. Reinhold Niebuhr has made this clear in his statement that "patriotism transmutes individual unselfishness into national egoism."[1] This same tendency is present in many limited loyalties. The lowest form of it may be "honor among thieves." In the case of the nation the object of loyalty is so inclusive and has such prestige that a patriotic person achieves moral satisfaction and the admiration of fellow citizens even though this loyalty may be used by the nation for exclusively egoistic purposes which are destructive in international relations.

This temptation within patriotism is strengthened by the capacity of a nation to enlist exalted moral idealisms in its own behalf. The nation generally identifies its interests with universal good or with the divine will. Thus any conflict between nations readily becomes a conflict between good and evil, between God and the devil. So much is this the case that Reinhold Niebuhr says that "perhaps the most significant moral characteristic of a nation is hypocrisy."[2] But he goes on to say that this hypocrisy is based in large part on self-deception. Our own nation has been able to convince most of its citizens that it was the guardian of democracy and freedom for the whole world. During the cold war it saw itself arrayed against Communism which was widely believed to be wholly evil, godless, and the enemy of freedom. The First World War, as we look back on it and compare it with the Second World War, was a conflict in which great issues were not at stake. But as soon as our country became a belligerent, the war became a crusade to make the world safe for democracy and a war to end war. George Kennan in writing about that war said the following: "There is, let me assure you, nothing in nature more egocentrical than an embattled democracy. It soon becomes the victim of its own propaganda. It then tends to attach to its own cause an absolute value which distorts its own vision on everything else. *Its* enemy becomes the embodiment of all evil. *Its* own side, on the other hand, is the center of all virtue."[3]

Within a nation's life there is a quite different source of ethical dilemmas. A government is responsible to a very mixed national community, which limits its range of moral choices. Its citizens have the most varied moral tendencies. In the United States many, Christians and non-Christians, are conscientious in their commitment to generous and humane goals for their nation in relation to other nations. Many others, however, have narrow nationalistic interests, or even more limited interests—especially economic—for which they seek governmental support. They may be responsive to the most chauvinistic propaganda. Many citizens are passive most of the time in relation to the kind of issues discussed in this book. But an indeterminate number of them can be influenced by the pressure of events and by leadership to support policies in the interest of peace and friendly relations with other countries. They may even be willing to make some sacrifices out of consideration for the needs of impoverished and hungry people abroad. Yet it is also true that leaders in government, when they would themselves choose a decent and wise policy, are often afraid of the possible backlash from the narrowly nationalistic part of the electorate. It is almost a rule that the most courageous decisions have to be postponed until after the next election!

We have summarized some of the reasons why decisions in international relations involve acute difficulties for those concerned about Christian ethics. There is always the temptation, as we have said, to try to keep ethics and international affairs in separate compartments. This is really an escape and it is ethically indefensible. Whether we choose it or not, the decisions with international consequences which we make as citizens, or to which we consent without protest, are morally a part of our lives. Attempted neutrality or plain default is a decision with consequences. If we try to do nothing, in effect we give support to the *status quo*, to those who now have the power.

THE GOD OF ALL NATIONS

When we see ourselves as citizens of our nation among the nations, we know that our God is the God of the whole world, of other nations as much as of the United States. This is where we should begin. God has no favorites among nations. God's love extends to all people. By God's righteousness all nations are judged.

The greatest temptation of any nation, especially one that has had a habit of making great claims for itself, is to identify itself with God. This may not take the form

of crude idolatry in which the nation overtly becomes
the object of worship. It is more likely to be the tendency
to assume that God is always on the side of our nation
because of its special virtue or because its cause is good.
Special claims have always been made for the American experiment—the original colonies and the new nation that was established. These claims had some truth
in them because at least what was happening on this
continent seemed to be a new beginning free from the
sins of the Old World, free from old conflicts, social
hierarchies, and many inherited incrustations. For example, John Adams said: "I always consider the settlement of America as the opening of a grand scheme and
design of Providence for the illumination of the igno-
rant and emancipation of the slavish part of mankind
all over the earth."[4] It is ironic that he used the word
"slavish." This reminds us that Adams and his col-
leagues, whether they believed in slavery or detested it
(as Adams did), could not keep this institution from
being incorporated into the structure of the new nation.
American spokesmen at their best, Abraham Lincoln
above all, were still able to see the new nation with all
of its promise as under judgment. Yet it is common for
our spokesmen to assume the superior virtue of our
country. Recently, President Gerald Ford said that
"America is morally and spiritually number one."[5]

When people think in vague terms of God as the Al-
mighty, it is easy to identify God with a mighty nation
that is assumed to be virtuous. But when God is believed
to be revealed in Jesus Christ, in the Biblical revelation
with Christ as the center, this idolatrous identification
of God with the nation becomes wholly incongruous.
The pride, vainglory, injustice, and cruelty of nations
stand out clearly in contrast to God as so revealed. The
very claims of Israel and Judah to be especially chosen
by God became grounds for the prophetic judgment. As
Amos said: "You only have I known of all the families

of the earth; therefore I will punish you for all your iniquities" (Amos 3:2). And then in The Book of Amos we have the remarkable leap in the prophetic understanding of God's universal rule: "Are you not like the Ethiopians to me, O people of Israel?" (ch. 9:7). Today there is a remarkable convergence of Christian interpreters, Protestant and Catholic, in support of the conviction that God is identified in a special way with people who are poor and oppressed. This says something important to the rich and powerful nations.

The love of God for all humanity (of which human love for all neighbors is a reflection) is an inspiration, a guide, and a source of judgment for churches and Christians as they relate themselves to the foreign policies of their nations. How far this guidance reaches to those who have no supporting religious convictions is a question that will always be in our minds as we write this book. One thing can be confidently said: This universal divine love indicates the solidarity of all humanity. From many different points of departure people discover this solidarity as a reality that determines their fate. The empirically discovered interdependence of all nations and peoples underlies the choices that nations must make whatever the controlling religious ideas may be. Hostility and vicious circles of vindictiveness among nations soon prove to be destructive of the welfare of the nations moved by them. Moreover, the global solidarity of nations makes it impossible to draw any line around the effects of such destruction. Reinhold Niebuhr, who is noted for his distrust of idealistic solutions of world problems, says in an essay on the illusions that he finds in such idealism: "Enlightened men in all nations have some sense of obligation to their fellow men, beyond the limits of their nation-state. There is at least an inchoate sense of obligation to the inchoate community of mankind."[6]

That may not seem to be much but it is where we must

start in tracing the effect of perceptions of the solidarity
of all nations on the ethical attitudes and judgments of
the citizens, Christian and non-Christian, of each nation. In this book we go far beyond this. We say in the
words of Pope Paul VI in his great encyclical *Populo-
rum Progressio:* "The rule which up to now held good
for the benefit of those nearest us, must today be applied
to all the needy of this world" (par. 49). Later chapters
will discuss how this way of thinking and feeling can
influence American policy.

One reminder of this Christian responsibility and also
a channel for its exercise is the membership of American Christians in the worldwide Christian community.
Christians are both citizens of nations and members of
this wider community. They should expect to experience some tension and even conflict between their role
as citizens and their role as members of the universal
church. Since the rise of nation-states, such conflict has
often been hidden by the tendency of churches, Protestant and Catholic, to give almost uncritical support to
national governments. Today there is no excuse for this,
for the larger church is more visible as a real community across national boundaries than at any time since
the Reformation.

The recent rapprochement between Protestants and
Roman Catholics in the world at large, and not least in
the United States, increases the opportunities of exposure to voices and influences and sources of religious
inspiration from beyond the nation. One illustration is
the fact that in many Latin-American countries the
Catholic Church through its leaders is struggling
against oppressive regimes that have the support of our
government and of American corporations. Were it not
for the courageous witness to human rights on the part
of Roman Catholics and a much smaller group of Protestants (the Catholic Church is so much the dominant

church), most of us in this country might have little awareness of what is taking place. One of the theological movements that has recently had most attention in the United States, the theology of liberation, has grown out of the suffering and the struggle of people in Latin America. To an important extent this struggle is seen by Latin-American theologians as struggle against the political and economic power of the United States as felt by their countries. Never before have Christian thinkers in Latin America received such attention in North America. One of the most prophetic Christian leaders in Latin America, Archbishop Helder Câmara of Brazil, is often in this country. Repeatedly he addresses Christians in the northern hemisphere about the injustice of having 20 percent of the world's people controlling 80 percent of the world's resources.

Wherever Christians fall into a hard nationalism that is indifferent to the needs of people in other countries or assumes that the peace of the world can best be served by the unilateral use of American power, they will hear from within the church how all that we are and do appears to people in other countries. This is especially true for countries where the effects of American governmental and corporate power are most acutely felt.

CHRISTIAN TEACHING ABOUT HUMANITY

So far we have been speaking of Christian obligations. Another dimension in Christian teaching describes at the deepest level the nature of people in the various nations. While there are many shades of theological interpretation between different traditions and schools of thought, there are two common elements in Christian teaching: One is the belief that all persons in all nations and of all races are created in the image of God. And the second is the realization that all people—and here it is especially important to make no exception in the case of oneself or one's own nation—are strongly inclined toward self-centeredness and pride. We shall consider the second conviction first. There has been much controversy between those who are hopeful about the best in human nature and those who consider themselves "realists" in their emphasis on the depth and pervasiveness of sin in the form of self-centeredness and pride. Our view is that we should not deduce from theological dogmas about sin any particular ideas about what is possible or impossible. Rather, we should take very seriously the implications of this side of Christian teaching. Think of the central place in Christian worship that repentance and confession are given in all Christian traditions. This should cause us to be realistic observers of the evidences of the strength of national self-centeredness and pride. We have already mentioned how the altruistic impulses of the individual are so easily steered into channels of national egoism. This egoism and pride may take the form of aggressive and interventionist policies or of economic imperialism. They may also take the form of isolationist indifference to the needs and sufferings of people who are on the other side of national boundaries. Pride may be expressed in blandness and self-satisfaction over national prosperity or virtue. In the case of a rich and powerful nation even these passive forms of self-centeredness and pride may have very destructive international consequences.

We see this negative side of humanity as an indication of the need for personal and national transformation. We see it also as a warning against expectations for utopian schemes or for total solutions of problems that do not take the stubbornness of national egoism into account. One emphasis in the teaching of those who have called themselves Christian realists needs to be taken seriously. It is the extent to which national self-righteousness supports hostility and contempt for other nations, aggravates conflicts, and often produces a hardness of heart that leads to policies that are aggressive and cruel. The cold war generated this kind of self-righteousness on both sides. Although reduced in intensity, these attitudes still distort the judgments of leaders and people on both sides.

Professor Herbert Butterfield, a British diplomatic historian and a lay theologian, greatly stresses the destructive role of national self-righteousness in history. While he is well aware of the sad fact that in many situations Christianity has stimulated self-righteousness, not least in the days of religious persecutions and of wars of religion, he believes that "Christianity alone attacks the seat of evil in the kind of world we have been considering, and has a solvent for the intellectual predicaments which arise in such a world. It addresses itself precisely to that crust of self-righteousness which, by the nature of its teaching, it has to dissolve before it can do anything else with a man." He goes on to say: "The more human beings are lacking in imagination, the more incapable men are of any profound kind of self-analysis, the more we shall find that their self-righteousness hardens, so that it is just the thick-skinned who are more sure of being right than anybody else. And though conflict may still be inevitable in history even if this particular evil did not exist, there can be no doubt that its presence multiplies all the deadlocks and gravely deepens all the tragedies of all the centuries."[7]

Perhaps the most telling statement of the warning against self-righteousness is the saying of Jesus: "Why do you see the speck that is in your brother's eye, but do not notice the log that is in your own eye?" (Matt. 7:3). Nations continually employ a double standard, judging other nations more harshly than themselves. Often we hear it said that morality has little place in international relations. But there is one place where we are sure to find abundant moral rhetoric and that is when nations denounce their adversaries in the name of righteousness.

Even more important is the other side of Christian teaching about humanity: all persons are made in the image of God. In the original Genesis passage this idea of the divine image is related specifically to the dominion of human beings over nature. This is true of the similar passage in Ps. 8. One implication of the Genesis passage is the equality of human beings in sharing the divine image as male and female. This conception of the image of God came to be the symbol for the promise, the dignity, and the greatness of humanity. This has been seen by various Christian thinkers as involving especially rationality, the social nature of persons, responsibility to God, and the capacity of people to transcend themselves through memory, imagination, and self-criticism. Theologians have had different ways of explaining the effect of the fall and original sin on this divine image. Always by some doctrinal route the positive aspect of humanity remains present, though there are many shades of optimism and pessimism concerning the resulting human situation.

For example, Karl Barth, often regarded as the greatest Protestant theologian of this century, in his basic theory seemed to allow the divine image in humanity to be destroyed by the fall. Still he came to the conclusion that the image of God had been restored by God's redemptive action in Christ, not only in the case of Christians but for humanity as a whole.

John Calvin, who is so well known for a doctrine of sin that seems devastating except for the elect, retained a positive view of humanity in the civil order and this would include international relations. In quite different ways Roman Catholicism and liberal Protestantism have preserved hopeful doctrines concerning the image of God in spite of the teaching about sin. Liberal Protestantism did tend to play down the sinful side of human nature and the tragic character of history. But correction at this point has come both from the ideas of Christian realism and from the experience of massive evil and of very deep and stubborn problems that do not go away.

In this book the assumption is made that all static and deterministic views of human sin are wrong. We cannot deduce from doctrines particular conclusions about what is possible or impossible in international relations. The image of God in humanity is always present in spite of the sinful human limitations that we have discussed. Since one of the chief evidences of these is our tendency toward self-righteousness, awareness of it enables us to detect in ourselves the obstacles to our perceiving the dignity and the possibilities of people in other nations.

All that we have said about the moral obligations involved in love for all neighbors without regard to national boundaries is strongly supported by this emphasis upon the divine image in them. It is a description of those to whom and for whom we have these moral obligations. The words of Jesus about loving our enemies may at first strike us as an obligation to be accepted in spite of the facts. Its meaning becomes entirely different when our deepest understanding of the facts is that the people who may happen to be enemies are made in God's image and are one with us. Translate all of this into political terms. Those distant people who live under the most unfamiliar cultural conditions and who are hungry or threatened by famine, those people on the other side of the ideological lines that divide humanity, those people at whom American missiles are now aimed, are made in God's image and are one with us. To have this vision is to be able to see beyond the immediate problems in the relations between nations to the essential humanity of all of us who are in the many nations, and to the possibilities of reconciliation and peace.

The two sides of Christian teaching about humanity should enable us to avoid both sentimental or romantic hopes for simple solutions of problems that have long been recalcitrant, and dogmatic pessimism, fatalism or cynicism.

MORALISM AND MORALITY

In a discussion of the relationship of ethics to international relations, an issue of immense importance is often raised. When nations emphasize moral goals they tend to be too rigid in their attitudes toward international conflicts and at times engage in destructive moral crusades. Our own country has often supported its use of power abroad with exaggerated claims of serving a moral cause, often the cause of democracy. This tendency, called "moralistic" by its critics, is often associated with Woodrow Wilson's view of America as the servant of international idealism. Moral absolutism has greatly intensified the conflicts of the cold war on both sides. The revulsion against our part in the war in Indochina, itself a consequence of the cold war, has encouraged criticism of moralism in foreign policy.

One of the strongest statements of this criticism was made in an article in 1971 by Arthur Schlesinger, Jr., under the surprising title "The Necessary Amorality of Foreign Affairs." Schlesinger says: "The compulsion to see foreign affairs in moral terms may have, with the noblest of intentions, the most ghastly consequences."[8]

One reason for this is that when a conflict between nations is turned into a matter of high moral principle, it is difficult for them to reach the kind of compromise that may be necessary if they are to live together in a dangerous world. Such high principles may be used to justify almost any means to secure victory for them. Both George Kennan and Hans Morgenthau have made a great deal of this destructive use of morality. As Morgenthau puts it: "What is good for the crusading nation is by definition good for all mankind, and if the rest of mankind refuses to accept such claims to universal recognition, it must be converted by fire and sword."[9] In contrast to this use of morality it is considered better for a nation to be governed by a wise view of its own interests rather than by moral idealism in foreign policy.

There is an important qualification in Schlesinger's thesis. He says in his article that moral values should be decisive "only in questions of last resort." And he adds that "questions of last resort exist."

There are, we believe, three ways in which morality should enter into the formation of foreign policy and into the relations between nations. It should determine the fundamental motives and attitudes of citizens and policymakers. Even the judgment that nations should avoid self-righteous crusading for absolute moral principles is a moral principle and presupposes attitudes of humility and restraint which are moral virtues. Concern for people as people everywhere, involving both respect and compassion, should always be present.

The second way in which morality should influence policy is in the criteria that determine immediate and long-range objectives. These objectives should be favorable to what we see to be universal good, but they should not be tied absolutely to the ideological slant from which we interpret that universal good. We have in mind such objectives as peace as the absence of war, which is no unimportant achievement in the world as it is, and peace as reconciliation between peoples, or economic justice between nations, or diversity and pluralism that enable nations to pursue their own political and social experiments, or the preservation of as wide an area in the world as possible in which ideas and information can circulate freely. I am sure that most critics of "moralism" in foreign policy would approve all of those objectives.

The third way in which morality should influence policy is that nations should accept moral limits on the means that they will use. George Kennan, who is one of the most insistent critics of moralism in international relations, says that "we should conduct ourselves at all times in such a way as to satisfy our own ideas of morality." He then says that we should "do this as a matter of obligation to ourselves and not as a matter of obligation to others."[10] That distinction seems to us to be artificial, but what Kennan means may be illustrated by his rejection as morally wrong the use of weapons of mass destruction as they were used in the Second World War against the populations of Dresden and Hamburg and later against the populations of Nagasaki and Hiroshima. He says: "I regret as an American and a Christian that these things were done." He adds: "If we must defend our homes, let us defend them as well as we can in the direct sense, but let us have no part in making millions of women and children and non-combatants hostages of the behavior of their governments."[11] It is hard to see how our obligation to ourselves to avoid doing wrong in our own eyes can be separated from concern for the victims of mass bombing.

We have recently had an example of a means used by our government which has generally been seen to be beyond all moral limits: the attempts by the CIA to assassinate foreign leaders. When the facts about this came to light there was a widespread moral revulsion against that practice. A good example was set in 1806 by the British foreign minister, Charles James Fox, who, when someone offered to assassinate Napoleon with whom his country was at war, was horrified and had the would-be assassin arrested and reported the incident to the French government.[12]

Hans Morgenthau's name is associated with a political realism that does not emphasize morality. Nevertheless, he speaks of the moral limits that nations should accept and which they often do. He notes that many nations reject the idea of mass killing in time of peace and says: "This limitation derives from an absolute moral principle, which must be obeyed regardless of national advantage." He calls attention to the fact that nations in recent decades have come to think differently in terms of morality about war, that war is morally condemned in principle, that nations seek to be free from the blame for starting a war. He says that there is strong moral condemnation for the very idea of engaging in preventive war "regardless of its expediency in view of the national interest."[13] It is extremely important to have such a moral consideration given priority over the national interest. In an article entitled "The Present Tragedy of America," Morgenthau greatly emphasizes the claims upon America of "the moral standards which it has set for itself." He recalls a discussion about Vietnam with a world-famous scientist who said to him: "You Americans don't know how we have looked to you as the last best hope, and now we feel betrayed." Morgenthau adds: "It is this betrayal, not only of the ethos of America but of the trust which, you may say, the best representatives of humanity have put in the United States, that constitutes the tragedy of America today."[14] We quote those words because they show that the attack on "moralism" by political realists is far from being an attack on morality as having a part in the policies of nations.

THE CLAIMS AND LIMITS OF PATRIOTISM

We shall conclude this discussion of the implications of Christian theology and ethics for international relations by considering the moral claims of patriotism. Should a Christian be a patriot or value patriotism as a virtue? We have called attention to the temptation that seems to be built into patriotism, for it so readily captures the altruism of the individual and turns it into the channel of national egoism. However, that is not the whole story. We believe that patriotism may be a great good if it remains subordinate to goods that are higher and wider. Patriotism generally springs from a deep emotion arising out of love for one's own people, for one's own homeland. There has been so much disillusionment in recent years growing out of a false glorification of America and out of the tragedies that have resulted from American pretensions that it seems necessary to say what the good is in patriotism.

Patriotism is love for our nearer neighbors, but it should not separate us from our more distant neighbors in other countries, nor should it prevent our caring for them. It is love for the community that surrounds us and from which we gain much of our identity. It is respect for its laws and institutions that have provided us with opportunities and securities usually taken for granted. Even minorities who have good reason to regard themselves as victims of some of our institutions can still appeal for changes in status and for opportunities to other institutions. Without being members of a particular community we would not be human, and it is not enough to belong only to some familial or local subcommunity. The national community stretches our horizons. It binds us to people of many types and conditions. Our American community is incredibly mixed and rich because of this diversity. Patriotism delivers us from the distortions that come from being controlled by much narrower loyalties, from seeing the world only from the point of view of the special groups or vested interests closest to us. Patriotism strengthens the motives of serving with integrity that part of the human community which we can most often reach in our daily lives.

Also, one's nation is the sphere in which people can most often have some part in decision-making, in influencing public opinion and public policy. American public policy has important international effects. Loyalty to the best in American traditions is an expression of patriotism. Often it can be expected to cause national policy to be beneficent if this loyalty is separated from false national pretensions, especially from efforts to impose the national will on other nations. To try to be a citizen of the world without caring for the national community that surrounds us is likely to mean escape from real people with whom we have vital relations into concern for humanity as an abstraction. This does not mean that we should have less concern for real human beings in other nations whom we never see.

Citizens of the United States may be thankful that our institutions make room for dissent—conscientious objection to military service, for example. Patriotism does not mean conformity to the will or to the ideals of those who happen to be in power. It is always proper to appeal to traditions, to a higher law embodied in the Constitution, especially the Bill of Rights, to protest a given policy. One unusual aspect of our history has been the role of religious movements committed to peace, such as the Quakers, the Mennonites, and the Church of the Brethren. Whether or not we agree with their absolute pacifism as a guide for policy, their witness to peace is a beneficent ingredient both in the witness of the American churches and in public opinion.

The American nation need not return to past forms of self-glorification, to pretentious and imperialistic conceptions of the national mission, in order to have a sense of national vocation. It is true to that vocation when it moves away from its present overemphasis on its military power, when it supports conditions of peace in the world, when it shows a special concern for those wider interests which it shares with other nations, when it is willing to accept limitations of sovereignty and to run risks to its security in the building of multilateral institutions of world order. Fortunately, in the very first sentence of the Declaration of Independence, there is that reference to "a decent respect to the opinions of mankind."

2

Inescapable Realities
in a Changing World

ANY MORAL WITNESS is always made within the environment of existing yet changing realities. Especially in this particularly dynamic period in history, past prescriptions for social improvement more quickly become dated. To be most effective in moving toward future goals of peace, justice, and freedom, foreign policy must now take into account a wide range of novel developments. As the systems approach indicates, changes in any part of the interrelated complex produces repercussions in all other parts.

To be sure, there are also important continuities in culture. For some time to come we will continue to share a heritage that includes nation-states, national interests, diplomatic conventions, and the existence of a United Nations and of numerous developing nations. In other respects the international realities to which we relate theological beliefs and ethical goals are sufficiently transformed by cumulative change that old prescriptions are no longer adequate for the intensified threats and enlarged opportunities that present themselves to this generation. Novel developments now introduce new urgencies and different problems, which require altered programs and priorities. In this chapter we will consider major aspects of the contemporary social situation that call for an updating of our ethical analysis of international affairs.

WEAPONRY AND WAR

For some time all of us have been belabored and be-
numbed by warnings about the increased destructive-
ness of military technology. Previous wars were tragi-
cally disruptive, but now we can destroy entire social
systems and threaten the continued existence of
humankind. We know that modern weaponry allows
people in rebellion against God to bring history to a
premature close. President John F. Kennedy said,
"Russia and the United States each now have enough
deliverable nuclear weapons to destroy the entire
human race several times over."[1] It is estimated that if
the firepower of current U.S. stockpiles of nuclear weapons was converted to TNT, it would fill a train of freight
cars stretching between the earth and the moon fifteen
times. Officials of both the United States and the Soviet
Union have publicly estimated up to 100 million deaths
on each side from the immediate blast and the resulting
fire storms of a nuclear exchange. Research continues
on new armaments, such as chemical and biological
weapons, death rays, or laser beams for killing and
knocking out equipment. It is likely to be only a question
of time until our present arsenals become old-fashioned
and comparatively inefficient instruments for reducing
this earth to an uninhabited ball of mud orbiting
through space.

We have not fully based international action on these
facts of modern existence partially because the threat of
reality was too great to hold in consciousness. A common psychological device for dealing with unmanageable anxiety is to repress it, to deny the existence of the
threat. We avoid exposure to information that substan-
tiates the threat, and wherever possible we interpret
information as though it promised security. Writing

with the background of a former president of the American Psychological Association, Charles E. Osgood said, "Seated in the backyard on a nice spring day, drinking a can of beer, watching the kids at play, and enjoying the trees and flowers, the Neanderthal within us simply cannot conceive of the trees blackened, the flowers suddenly withered, and the voices of the children stilled—or there being no more beer."[2]

Even worse, the repressed, unconscious anxiety can still force its way out in dangerous symptoms, as, for example, in the irrational compulsion to try out the threatening situation in an attempt to prove that it will not lead to calamity. We therefore play with fire, or indulge in the international equivalent of highway games of "chicken." The only positive way to deal with modern military technology is to look openly and directly at its frightful mien and to work at a solution to the problem it creates, thus channeling fear into constructive action.

Such a mature, conscious attention to our dilemma would alter our foreign policy considerably. Over the past centuries it has been argued that war, even with its tragic consequences, may still be defended when more is gained than is lost. This argument now applies much less often than it once did. Now that the devastation of war is so much greater and the range of values it destroys is so much wider, fewer types of war can be responsibly debated as possible rational instruments of national policy. Wars on vital issues between great powers have lost their credibility, as leaders of both the United States and the Soviet Union have openly indicated. Only the most limited of wars with little probability of escalation are legitimately to be considered as perhaps becoming rational instruments of national policy.

A far-reaching consequence is that traditional policies of containment or of alliances are no longer adequate. As Hans Morgenthau has pointed out, our alliances with nations ringing the boundaries of the Soviet and Chinese empires may signal our resolution, but "they have no direct military relevance in a nuclear setting, save as additional targets for nuclear attack."[3] Missiles can fly over the top of our conventional rings of steel once forged to contain another nation. Policies that may have been appropriate for former times are no longer adequate in a nuclear setting. For defusing aggression and exploitation in contemporary times new approaches that move significantly beyond traditional military alliances between sovereign states are required.

POLITICAL REALITIES

The world continues to be divided into separate nation-states. The sovereignty that each claims can be defined as legal nonaccountability, or as the possession of supreme coercive power. Political states assert authority over all organizations within their boundaries, but they recognize no authority outside themselves over their own acts. The only treaties or controls that a sovereign state accepts are those which the state itself adopts. In cases of disagreement between nations when neither is willing to change its position, the only alternative is a contest of power, with war still the last resort. This is still an appeal to might in an effort to determine the right. Separate sovereign states are both interdependent and mutually threatening. The strength of one becomes the insecurity of others.

Especially in the absence of available alternatives there are important reasons that separate states still retain most of the decision-making power they now claim. As was pointed out in the preceding chapter, citizens do owe an appropriate patriotic allegiance to deserving governments. Proper expressions of patriotism are part of any professed allegiance to God and to the welfare of humankind. But insofar as national sovereignty remains a claim to absolute and unconditional supremacy, it can become, as Robert Heilbroner once put it, "a kind of secular church in an age without religion."[4] To this the Christian must object, both because of a primary allegiance to God and because of the realities of the modern world.

New technologies have transnational consequences that increasingly raise serious questions about the adequacy of the existing state system. Intercontinental travel is ever faster and cheaper. Improved technology invites new forms of criminal activity across national boundaries, for example, airplane hijackings or narcotics smuggling. Communication by earth-orbiting satellites demands decisions about who shall own them, how the preferred positions are to be allocated, and what intrusions across national boundaries become a new form of invasion. Nation-states cannot separately cope with such emerging problems.

Fragmentation of an increasingly interdependent world has been a perennial difficulty. Now that the areas of interdependence have become so crucial, essentially unrestrained or anarchistic action by completely autonomous states has become intolerable. Some of the major functions traditionally assigned by Christian theologians to political authority can no longer be performed by separate nation-states. A single nation cannot now preserve peace, freedom, or security for its citizens when other nations can invade by missiles or disrupt by terrorism. Justice and opportunity are no longer isolated matters when the economic policy of one country can depress and disrupt the economies of many others. The security and welfare of all become a necessary prerequisite to the security and welfare of each.

It is a basic insistence of democracy that all those

whose welfare is vitally affected by an important decision have a right to a voice and a vote in making that decision. The goals of cooperation and community which have been projected by our religious insight must now become the dimensions of political organization. God's unification of humankind in God's creation and universal concern must now increasingly become a fact in our social structures. This will involve some form of international organization with final power for decision within an area limited enough that no state could be destroyed, yet broad enough to liberate the full possibilities in the increased interdependency among nations.

The dynamics of modern civilization dictate a greater reliance on international organization and less of a sole dependence on national power. This is becoming increasingly essential to the long-run highest welfare of all. The nation-state is increasingly obsolescent as the sole repository of sovereignty. As Norman Cousins has put it: "The compression of the whole of humanity into a single geographic arena is the signal event of the contemporary era. The central question of that arena is whether the world will become a community or a wasteland, a single habitat or a single battlefield."[5]

The growing interpenetration of societies may provide a better basis for international cooperation than we had in the days when commercial interdependence was practically the only tie between nations. Now a growing cosmopolitanism is gradually providing more transnational social relationships and loyalties. More persons now feel a more intense identification with worldwide science, scholarship, business, and athletics. We now need international organization not only to avoid the perils of war but also to facilitate the gains of a more comprehensive cultural exchange. There are greater dangers than ever before in separation of the nations and more benefits to be had by cooperation than in any previous period.

The need for international structures for growing interdependence has been becoming apparent for some time. This need is reinforced by at least two recent trends toward cultural pluralism, both of which tend to undermine the authority of the nation-state and to strengthen the case for international action. One of these in industrial countries is the growing alienation from the dominant mores of an affluent society. This protest against the establishment has spread to numerous countries. A greater sense of international affinity may develop among countercultural protestors against materialism, bureaucracy, and the suppression of the individual. Even though such a transformation of lifestyle may not soon become the dominant culture, the transnational bond between those sharing the same values may still become stronger as the authority of the nation-state weakens. We have already seen a somewhat similar historic precedent in the international impact of Marxism and of Christianity. A growing number of people are responding to relationships not only vertically to a variety of social groups within a single geographical and political territory but also horizontally to similar cultural groups in many different nations.

The ability of nation-states to command the loyalty and affection of their citizens is also eroding before the current rise of ethnicity. Deprived classes have sometimes in the past felt comparatively stronger ties across national boundaries. Now those who share common ethnic ties are showing similar reactions. Especially when they feel themselves economically or politically deprived within a particular state, they are demanding greater autonomy and seeking help from similar groups in other countries. Catholics in Northern Ireland, Jews in the Soviet Union, blacks in the United States, or Palestinians in Israel become illustrations. Some of these groups would rejoice at the defeat of their existing homeland if it contributed to victory for their ethnic vision of community. Traditional international patterns of balance of power, bipolarity, or even the redrawing of national boundaries are no longer sufficient to deal with this driving concern for a new pluralism. Will the outcome be self-determination in smaller states that join in international union for desirable economic and political purposes? Or will this driving force be satisfied by international guarantees of the rights of ethnic groups within existing nations? Will ethnicity be subordinated in a pluralistic pattern within a common humanity? Whichever of these may be the outcome (or a combination of various such solutions) it is clear that we face a demand for redistribution of wealth and power in the modern world, as well as a demand for security in peace. Neither of these goals can be fully realized except under international auspices.

ECONOMIC FACTORS

Economic competition has always placed a major strain on harmonious relationships between countries. National boundary lines have been drawn across a globe that has resources unevenly distributed. This fact alone produces have and have-not nations, depending on how much arable land, mineral resources, or other sources of wealth lie within a country's borders. Historical circumstances and cultural differences have intensified the dilemmas. Now new factors that greatly alter our international problem are being added.

The revolt of the disprivileged is being intensified. More persons in the hinterlands of the world are hearing about the affluence of a minority of humankind. Even in the poverty areas where standards of living are rising, discontent may thereby be intensified. Revolutions are the product not so much of dismal despair as of too slowly improving circumstances, as peoples sense the possibility of hope, only to have it frustrated. It is *relative* deprivation that is the important consideration in the fire storm of exploding expectations sweeping the world. With all that we have done, the gap is widening. Although the plight of the poorest has improved, that of the rich has improved even faster. Even though two economies were both growing at the same percentage rate, the gap could still be widening if the base to which the same percentage of growth was added was a great deal more in one country than in the other. We have been forced to recognize how complex and far-reaching the necessary changes are, and how weak and quickly exhausted the moral resources of the wealthy are.

As some materials are coming into scarce supply, the weak are learning to combine into cartels against the strong or to play one superpower against another. No loftier a motivation than self-interest has introduced into recent foreign policy elements that would not have been seriously considered even a short time ago. There are few, if any, serious economic problems we now face that are not partly effected by world conditions and require global treatment. Stimulation of economic growth and human development, and the prevention of energy shortages, business recession, inflation, and environmental pollution all require forms of international cooperation which we have traditionally hesitated to adopt. We are now in a situation where caring for the interests of our own nation forces us to care for the interests of the world.

The economic face of the earth has also been changed by the increased strength of multinational corporations. While these gigantic complexes offer some new opportunities for international cooperation, they also raise serious new questions for foreign policy. Transnational corporations make a greater impact on the life of humanity than do many nation-states. Yet in some respects they can operate outside the laws of all nation-states. Huge "cosmocorps" can dominate small states, exploiting or developing their economies and undermining or supporting their legitimate governments. Tax havens can also become pollution havens when factories are moved to countries with less stringent laws for environmental protection. By transferring operations, multinational corporations can frustrate regulation by even powerful nations. Financial dealings can be so arranged as to avoid domestic taxation and monetary controls. To stabilize and stimulate the economy, nations have used various fiscal and production policies, but corporations with such massive economic resources can bypass national economic policies, thus making them considerably less effective. Thereby governments lose some of their sovereignty to small private interest groups. Who then is to control the private interests involved for the sake of the common good? Part of the answer must be found in international regulations —a new departure in international affairs necessary to deal with unprecedented dilemmas.

New demands on the ingenuity of humankind are now also being made by the increasing use of oceans and of outer space. New factors emerging in these enlargements of the human environment carry lethal possibilities along with progressive capabilities.

Outer space holds potentialities that strain even the imagination of science fiction. Who knows what the possibility of satellites and even space travel may be for peacetime development? When American and Russian astronauts supported each other in maneuvers in outer space, they illustrated new dimensions of international cooperation. At the same time, however, both the United States and the Soviet Union have been developing space programs for military purposes. Satellites can be used for communication or weather prediction; they can also become spies in the sky. They can provide increased accuracy in guiding missiles to targets on earth, or they may become launching pads for fighting wars in outer space. The militarization of space holds devastating possibilities for destruction. It would also mine out more of the earth's essential resources for military hardware which would finally be left as junk far above the earth. The 1967 UN outer space treaty, ratified by both the United States and the Soviet Union, specifies that outer space shall be explored and used "in the interest of all countries" and that outer space "shall be the province of all mankind." In general terms, the treaty forbids placing "weapons of mass destruction" into orbit. This is only a beginning, however. We do not yet have adequate controls to ensure observance of these principles, especially when the pressure to violate them becomes great. Major effort along innovative lines is required if outer space is not to become an unprecedented battleground.

The oceans of the world have in the past been open to all. Now they may also become a new battlefield as well as a new environmental threat to the human race. Recent technological developments foreshadow the mining of the seabed. There are valuable manganese nodules lying on the ocean floor, and other sources of hard minerals under the ocean floor. Offshore oil becomes especially attractive as other sources become more nearly exhausted. It has been estimated that offshore petroleum reserves are greater than those under dry land. We may soon experience vast land grabs enforced by navies, planes, and missiles. Will the nations that can afford it play "winner take all" in a new form of worldwide colonialism? Such a resurgence of imperialism would produce bitter fruit. On the other hand, if ocean development took place under international auspices, taxes paid by ocean enterprises could support strong UN programs for keeping the peace, protecting the environment, and aiding poor countries. At the moment, however, the technology of ocean mining is outstripping the politics of ocean control.

Conflict over world fishing rights poses similar dangers. There is a growing tendency for nations with ocean frontage to push their territorial claims farther out to sea, for example, from a 3-mile limit to a 200-mile limit. This is triggering sharp conflicts over fishing rights, as in the "cod war" between Iceland and England, or in the seizure of U.S. fishing vessels off the coast of South America. Related to this are reports of such over-fishing as to threaten the reproductive capacity and therefore the world's supply of food fish. Who will monitor fishing and prevent conflict over fishing rights? Will the sea be shared and protected? Realistic answers at the moment must be pessimistic. New rules for ocean use must be formulated if we are to avoid widespread conflict and if we are to conserve rich deposits of resources for those who have a rightful claim, namely, all the peoples of the world.

ECOLOGICAL ASPECTS

Only recently have we become seriously aware of the relationship between foreign policy and the ecological environment necessary to sustain human life. To the destructive potentialities of nuclear weapons must now be added other forms of pollution and resource exhaustion in relationship to growing populations.

The activities of individual nations can undermine life supports for everyone in the world. A single nation may consider it to be in its own interests to continue its current consumption of energy, for example. But when many nations pursue similar interests, no nation can achieve its ends. There are not enough resources to go around. Growing world shortages in vital materials will increase competitive pressures between nations. There will be increased desires to dominate territorial sources of scarce items. Conflicts between rich and poor nations will be intensified. Arms races will be accelerated. As a Swedish proverb puts it, "When the feedbox is empty the horses bite each other."

The "fat man theory" maintains that as a country like the Soviet Union becomes more affluent, it also becomes more conservative and less troublesome internationally. It is also true that as fat nations try to maintain their standards of living in a world of greater resource scarcity, they may become more defensive, imperialistic, and belligerent. On the other hand, if we accurately see the dimensions of the ecological threat, the nations of the world may be brought closer together in cooperative action to meet the common problem. Environmental collapse, like the possibility of nuclear war, could be seen as the equivalent of an invasion from Mars, bringing all nations together in a grand alliance of earthlings. Crisis can contribute to more rapid progress, but this more fortunate outcome depends on moral resources of sensitivity and altruism, and on a predisposing public opinion on political and economic matters which points us toward creative rather than self-defeating policies. It is doubtful whether we now have either set of resources.

In view of the total ecological picture, we should be more resentful of the resources wasted in war and preparation for war. Armaments are environmentally destructive even if they are never used in combat. A major source of resource depletion is arms manufacture.

The realities of our planet include not only finite resources but also limited pollution-absorbing capacity. For example, polluted rivers pour into the ocean, which is a big lake without an outlet. Ocean pollution can upset the delicate balance on which life everywhere depends. If we continue to use the ocean as a huge septic tank for our sewage, including pesticides and industrial wastes, we are likely in the long run to affect the ocean's role in photosynthetic activity, carbon dioxide absorption, and climate control. Already the Mediterranean is, in the words of Seyom Brown, "practically choking to death for want of multinational ecological care."[6] In the not too distant future the question may be whether we can still get enough oxygen to breathe.

Another environmental threat emerges from increasing reliance on nuclear power plants for meeting growing energy demands. Large quantities of plutonium are involved, and dangerous wastes have to be disposed of. If plutonium is not safely handled, its lethal effects can be widespread. According to Mihajlo Mesarovič and Eduard Pestel, "A ball of plutonium the size of a grapefruit contains enough poison to kill nearly all of the people living today."[7] When a mishap can poison adjacent lands and populations for thousands of years, what would a country do if its neighbor had inadequate security provisions in its nuclear reactors? How would a nation safeguard its people in case of turmoil, civil war, or irresponsible leadership in a nearby land? Criminals or revolutionary terrorists may hijack loads of fissionable material or release nuclear wastes from storage vaults. Some feel that even a few persons might storm a nuclear power plant, place explosives near a critical safety feature, and threaten to send radioactive particles drifting over nearby areas. As the nuclear industry grows, the threat of nuclear theft, sabotage, and blackmail is likely also to become more serious. In a world sharply divided between rich and poor, the motivation of rational persons for such terrorism is also likely to grow—at the same time that the potentialities for neurotic action remain great. As James M. Wall put it, "While most of us are worried that someone could kill the President of the United States with a small handgun, a number of scientists in our midst are troubled over the possibility that one disturbed individual could steal a few pounds of plutonium and blow up the world."[8]

Furthermore, the ozone in the atmosphere is necessary to protect living things against ultraviolet rays. The release of certain chemicals can damage the earth's ozone shield. The testing of thermonuclear bombs is reported already to have resulted in what may be an irreversible loss of ozone. These weapons tests represent only a minute part of the megatonnage of current nuclear stockpiles. The use of our existing weapons capacity might well destroy an effective ozone shield. Norman Cousins concludes, "Under these circumstances, even the possession of nuclear explosives is an explicit crime against humanity and should clearly be recognized as such by world public opinion."[9]

Although we do not yet know as much about these matters as we would like, informed scholars are concerned about the effects on the earth's heat balance of human activities like industrial combustion of fossil fuels and deforestation. The accumulation of carbon dioxide in the atmosphere might create a "greenhouse effect," trapping more heat near the earth's surface, thus melting the polar ice caps. This would result in both a flooding of some major land masses and the turning of others into deserts too hot for habitation.

Certainly it is clear that every human being is ecologically joined to every other person in common dependence on the biosphere. Humanity rides in the same fragile lifeboat, and no section of the boat is safeguarded by drilling larger holes in the enemy's section than the enemy is drilling in ours. There is no longer a "fortress America" to protect us in isolation. Confining action to separate sovereign states is no longer compatible with our physical interdependence. Depletion of resources, pollution, and destruction of the ecological balance require global action beyond that of existing national governments. The threat of environmental collapse, along with dangers in nuclear war and economic breakdown, should be a powerful stimulus to such international action. Much in our past policy has now become both obsolete and suicidal.

3

Experts, Policymakers, and Absolutists

FEW READERS are likely to doubt that there are moral issues at stake in international relations. Most will agree that the churches have responsibility to help their members discover significant moral landmarks that should guide them in making their own decisions in regard to foreign policy. There are some goals to be sought and wrong paths to be avoided. The church should help the nation to resolve to seek the one and to reject the other. But after all these things are said, the most difficult problems remain. Issues and choices in regard to what should be done by governments in international relations are often highly complex and their complexity involves elements that are the subject of this chapter.

We may find that two goals which have a moral claim are in conflict or at least in tension with each other. One may have to be subordinated to another, and even those persons who are most concerned about the ethical aspects of international relations may find themselves on opposite sides of important decisions. In abstract terms the goals in conflict may be peace and freedom, or peace and justice. Sometimes there may be a conflict of goals, such as stability in some part of the world and the good that is at stake in revolutionary struggles for justice. For two decades after the Second World War, American foreign policy had two goals though there were important differences of emphasis in regard to them both, in the American churches and in the nation. One was the containment of Communism which was regarded as a threat to the freedom of many countries. One dimension of this threat was through military attack, thought to be a possibility in Europe; the other was through support of subversive or revolutionary forces within nations which was believed to be the danger especially in Asia, Africa, and Latin America. The other goal was the prevention of a third world war. Since such a war would involve the two great nuclear powers it was assumed by the policymakers in both that peace was best served by possessing enough nuclear power for each to deter the other.

There could be honest differences of opinion between those who regarded the containment of Communism as a less fateful goal than the prevention of nuclear war and those who held the opposite opinion. Two decades ago there was much talk about how much better it would be to be "dead than red." We began to hear less of this when it came to be realized that there are many shades of "red." Also, there is today an honest difference of opinion between those who are confident that nuclear deterrence will prevent nuclear war and those who believe that, though this may have been true for a time and may still be true, it becomes increasingly a doubtful road to peace. On both of these issues lines may be formed differently than they were before the radical split in international Communism and before the war in Vietnam. But these conflicting emphases still remain, and we believe these differences do divide people of equal moral sensitivity. Those who are certain that any use of military force is morally wrong may question that statement. For the most part, however, the long debates that we have had between pacifists and non-pacifists have overcome the tendency for either side to deny full sincerity and moral sensitivity to the other. Each also recognizes that the other makes errors in judgment. It is moral dilemmas of this sort that in practice turn out to be the heart of the moral problems encountered in international relations.

THE NECESSITY AND LIMITS OF SPECIALIZED EXPERTISE

International issues are complex because some aspects of them are technical. It is essential that the judgments of experts as well as the judgments of moralists be related to decision-making. They are complex because they are not only moral and technical but also political. This is true in two ways. They are political because what our own government is able to do depends on public opinion within the nation, upon elections, and sometimes upon the outcome of struggles between Congress and the executive. Foreign policy decisions should be discussed in election campaigns, but often they become emotional issues demagogically used to win votes. Candidates are pushed into false positions and the public is confused. Foreign policy issues are also political issues because what can be done depends upon the political situation in other nations, upon the state of international organizations, upon broad trends of opinion. Feelings of resentment or aspiration in large parts of the world have an effect. There are experts who can throw light on these matters but often they can offer little more than educated guesses.

When international political issues become entangled with questions of military security, military specialists who can estimate the effect of any decision on the relative military strength of nations must play their part. Often they are taken too seriously as experts concerning political matters and the *intentions* of other nations. When international political issues are related to economic conflicts, to the problems of rich and poor, of hunger, or of corporate power that is independent of governments, economists and sociologists and agriculturalists and many other experts will have contributions to make. Today agriculturalists are often the most important experts for key issues of foreign policy.

We need to comment especially on the place of the expertise of those who are specialists in international relations. They have had great influence on American foreign policy since the Second World War. In three cases men who had claim to this kind of expertise became secretaries of state: John Foster Dulles, Dean Rusk, and Henry Kissinger. Though not as much a specialist as those three, Dean Acheson should also be included. We have cited two experts in Chapter 1 (George Kennan and Hans Morgenthau) who have had great prestige as writers but less power. Also Reinhold Niebuhr, whom we have quoted, though primarily a theologian, has been an adviser to foreign policymakers. George Kennan, as chairman of the State Department planning committee for which he had gathered together a number of experts, said of Niebuhr that he was the "father of us all."

These experts have not all agreed on the importance of the military factor in the cold war or about the wisdom or moral justification of America's role in Indochina. The secretaries of state whom I have named have all been architects of different phases of our Indochina policy. Except for Kissinger's support of détente with the Soviet Union and China, they were all quite belligerent in their anti-Communism with a strong emphasis on the military approach to the cold war. Acheson and Dulles both advocated military support for the French in Indochina in the 1950's. Kissinger took four years after he became a major policymaker to bring the American role in the war to an end. Even after adopting a policy of détente toward the great Communist powers he continued to support an interventionist anti-Communist policy in the Third World in Chile and Angola, and in Western Europe in Portugal and Italy.

There has been a concentration of foreign policy experts around the Council on Foreign Relations in New York. Academic experts, publicists, and many political figures join the leaders of business and finance in discussing international relations. The official organ of the Council is *Foreign Affairs,* a journal of great prestige, though it is often criticized for having reflected one-sidedly a consensus that has dominated American foreign policy since the Second World War. In the main this has been a fair criticism, but today this consensus no longer exists. The Indochina war which caused convulsions in American public opinion destroyed this consensus both among experts and among those close to policymaking.

Six years ago another quarterly was founded called *Foreign Policy* which has support from a diverse group of experts in the field. For the most part it represents a fresh, postconsensus outlook on issues of foreign policy. Though its sponsors overlap with those of *Foreign Affairs,* its articles reflect the need for quite new choices in relation to both the East-West and the North-South tensions in the world. To the left of both of these journals and the groups supporting them are the experts connected with the Institute of Policy Studies out of which have come several books. Richard J. Barnet's *The Roots of War*[1] is a radical criticism of the "national security bureaucracy" that has controlled policy in recent decades. *Global Reach,*[2] written by him with Ronald E. Müller, is one of the ablest and most drastic criticisms of the multinational corporations and their effect on the nations of the Third World.

The passing of generations, the changes among Com-

munist nations, the recent recognition of the high priority of problems of justice between rich and poor nations,
and especially the trauma of the Indochina war have
created a new situation. A much more diversified expertise should now be made available to government. The
opening up of China, the rehabilitation of many of the
older experts on China who had been victims of Joseph
McCarthy's persecutions, and a new generation of Asia
scholars have greatly changed the picture. Fear of
China and ignorance about China resulting from
McCarthy's discrediting of those who knew most about
it were a blight on American foreign policy for two
decades and had much to do with our involvement in
the Indochina war. One ground for hope as we face the
future is that public opinion about China during the
1960's began to change. Richard Nixon, in his days of
greatest trouble, was still given credit by most Americans for reopening relations with China. Even when
public opinion appears to be very much hardened it can
quickly change.

David Halberstam in his *The Best and the Brightest*[3]
popularized the idea that the men most responsible for
our involvement in the Indochina war were liberal intellectuals, products of the best Eastern universities,
men who had the experience of forming foreign policy
during and after the Second World War. This was a time
when the United States was clearly the dominant power
in the world and came to expect to have its way in Asia
as had been the case in Europe at the war's end. Power,
military and economic, and the giddiness that came
from success were the background of the foreign policy
consensus to which we have referred.

A younger expert who for a time did participate in
that consensus and whose associations were with its
chief academic representatives has written out of his
own experience about the enormous change that has

taken place among the foreign policy experts. Zbigniew Brzezinski, National Security Adviser in the Carter Administration and formerly a State Department adviser under President Johnson, is a much admired academic expert on the Communist nations. He has published an article in *Foreign Policy* that shows his own independence of the foreign policy establishment with which he had been associated. He says that the consensus of which we have spoken was that of "a WASP elite" which had "the cold war as the basic organizing principle." He also attributes to it the tendency "to assign higher priority to external obligations than to internal needs." About the eroding of the establishment that long dominated policy he says: "The waning of the WASP-eastern seaboard-Ivy League-Wall Street foreign affairs elite is a critically important aspect of that change. That elite, dominant in foreign affairs for more than half a century, provided the country with much of its leadership during America's thrust to world greatness, and that leadership was in turn based on shared values and solid institutional pillars of support."[4] That is a remarkable statement because it comes from one who engages neither in popular journalism nor in simplistic political propaganda. It is from a scholar who, while not a WASP in origin, seemed to be one of the most brilliant members of the very group whose waning influence he describes.

The motives of those who belonged to this group deserve comment. Their association with the leaders of business and finance had much to do with their interest in preserving American hegemony in the world and of keeping as many doors as possible open on all continents for American business. Those who rewrite the history of the postwar period from what is called a "revisionist" point of view seize upon this interest to define the meaning of all that happened during the period of the cold war. The cold war itself they regard as chiefly made in Washington and New York. (See, e.g., Joyce and Gabriel Kolko, *The Limits of Power: The World and United States Foreign Policy, 1945–1954;* Harper & Row, Publishers, Inc., 1972.) It is difficult to preserve one's balance on this issue, and some of our readers may think that the last thing we want today is balance! We have no intention of playing down the strong motives that caused policymakers to oppose Communism as an economic system that was hostile to capitalism. Nor do we fail to understand why they did what they could to preserve the availability to the United States of raw materials, markets for American goods, and opportunities for American investments. Also persons who had most influence on foreign policy were as outraged by the enormities of Stalinism as they had been by Hitlerism. They feared that the free world would be reduced by Communist power closing in on it from both east and west.

It is difficult today to reconstruct how the world appeared to Americans who saw all the values they cherished, not only economic, threatened by a united international Communist power with major bases in both the Soviet Union and China, with the Soviet Union becoming our equal in military power. In this context many Americans believed that the Communists should not be allowed to take over another square mile of territory. The fear of changes in the *status quo* that favored leftist movements which might be instruments of Communism or vulnerable to Communist influence became an obsession. "Stability"—not "justice," not even "freedom," but "stability"—became the great word. It is essential to understand this situation which prevailed in the late '40s and early '50s to grasp what it was that moved policymakers and experts until the late '60s. Their minds were formed in that earlier period. Neither the death of Stalin nor the breakup of international Communism and the coming into existence of many Communisms changed their minds. Only our failure in Indochina and the profound split in this country over the war began to cause reassessment of America's role in the world.

Our interest in reviewing this development is to indicate that these policymakers who are now so much criticized were not without moral concerns. They shared the purpose expressed by Dean Acheson: "To preserve and foster an environment in which free societies may exist and flourish." In doing so they helped to build up many unfree societies which were believed to be less of a threat to existing free societies than the major Communist powers. In the course of the Indochina war they lost all moral sense of proportion about means. The words about the destruction of one village came to describe their whole strategy in Indochina: "We destroyed the village in order to save it." This was the irony and also the tragedy of American policy. The experts were proved wrong by events.

Whenever we deal with any kind of experts in the political or social sciences it is important to consider not only the contribution of their superior knowledge but also the presuppositions that determine their use of that knowledge. This is no plea for an anti-intellectual carelessness about knowledge. Some of those who are critics of the experts may be partisans without knowledge, purveyors of a destructive demagoguery or of an irrelevant idealism. One protection is to be exposed to a variety of experts with different presuppositions. In economics no amount of expertise can overcome the differences between those who assume that the free-enterprise system will correct itself if the government greatly reduces its interference, and those who believe that to leave the system to its own processes of self-correction would make victims of so many people that the government should intervene to protect them. It is not greater or lesser expertise that can explain the differences on this issue in economics between a Milton Friedman and a John Kenneth Galbraith. In international relations what the experts see depends upon important assumptions they make about this period of history: assumptions about the rival claims of justice and stability, assumptions about the range of American responsibilities and the limits of American power, assumptions about the nature of Communism and about the role and intentions of Communist nations, assumptions about the relevance and the efficacy of military power in achieving objectives, not to speak of assumptions about the moral limits to its use, assumptions about the influence of nationalism in nations that have recently become independent, assumptions about the extent to which American business activities abroad can be constructive in relation to the economic welfare of the people most affected by them, assumptions about how best to prevent a third world war. We doubt if these assumptions can themselves be seen primarily as the result of scientific expertise, though they may be influenced by it. Still they determine the kind of recommendations in regard to policy the expert makes, and his or her reputation as an expert gives prestige to the recommendations.

POLICYMAKERS AND CITIZENS

A significant illustration of the way experts and policymakers view the role of morality occurs in a famous speech made at Amherst College in 1964 by Dean Acheson. Mr. Acheson was a major architect of the Marshall Plan, one of the most constructive American contributions to international relations since the Second

World War. This speech gave the impression that Acheson was discounting morality because he criticized particular positions often regarded as *the* moral positions. He said that "the vocabulary of morals and ethics is inadequate to discuss or test foreign policy of states." One reason for this is that "what a government can and should do with the resources which it takes from its citizens must be governed by wholly different considerations from those which properly determine an individual's use of his own." Certainly those who make decisions for government cannot spend public money guided only or chiefly by their private idealisms. Acheson says that the overriding guide for the policymaker is "strategic." By this he means that he or she must determine how effectively policy will achieve a major national goal. We have already cited Acheson's definition of a national goal: "creating an environment in which free societies may flourish." This is a moral goal. It is one-sided, reflecting the American ideological emphasis on freedom as contrasted with justice, and it needs to be subjected to moral criticism. But it is neither amoral nor immoral.

Another point at which morality enters into Acheson's calculations appears when he discusses means and ends: "If you object that this [the strategic approach] is no different from saying that the end justifies the means, I must answer that in foreign affairs only the end can justify the means; that this is not to say that the end justifies any means, or that some ends can justify anything." His illustration of unjustified means is taken from the behavior of Italian city-states in the fifteenth century. He might have chosen an illustration nearer home! The principle is clear: morality does set limits to means.

One doubtful statement in Acheson's speech is important if moral criticism of means is permitted to enter into the discussion of decision-makers who are on the spot and who face options of great difficulty. He says that "those involved in the Cuban missile crisis of October, 1962, will remember the irrelevance of the supposed moral considerations brought out in the discussion." Robert Kennedy in his book *Thirteen Days*[5] gives a firsthand account of the discussion in the small inside group that made the decision to quarantine Cuba rather than to attack the Cuban bases from the air, which several members of the group favored, or to invade Cuba. It is significant that the military members of the group favored both an air strike and an invasion! Kennedy himself helped to shift the opinion of the group by saying that an air strike against Cuba would be against our own moral traditions as a nation. George Ball also maintained this view. Acheson, who was present, opposed it and yet this view had an effect on the thinking of the group. Arthur Schlesinger, Jr., in a later account of the discussion says: "In retrospect most participants regarded Robert Kennedy's speech as the turning point."[6] This is an example of decision-makers facing a dreadful dilemma and whose intimate discussion is to a considerable extent a matter of record. It is a great loss that Robert Kennedy did not live to answer the prior question which he hoped to write about later: "What, if any, circumstances or justification gives this government or any government the moral right to bring its people or possibly all people under the shadow of nuclear destruction?"

Acheson was primarily a policymaker. Policymakers often acquire a measure of expertise. In a negotiating situation they may know what the nuances of the situation are better than anyone else. Also, they are on the spot. They are forced to come to conclusions, to say yes or no *now* to a question about immediate action. This stimulates the mind, and this kind of forced option may be a source of wisdom that is not available to the detached expert. It may also lead to foolish and deplorable action. The episode of the Cuban missile crisis is an excellent example of being on the spot. The policymaker also has to live with the results of his decision. This may make him more wisely cautious than the detached expert. It may also lead him to be too cautious about the political effects on his career.

To be a policymaker by no means assures that a person will be wiser or more morally sensitive. Often it has the reverse effect when a policymaker comes to have a vested interest in a particular policy. He has really gambled on it and it has become associated with his name, and he may continue in what to others seems a disastrous course in order to prove finally that he was right. Many policymakers from presidents down had such a vested interest in the American role in the Indochina war which caused them to be rigid in their opposition to all criticism. (We have not said "he or she" in this context, because American policy has suffered from being almost exclusively dominated by men!)

Professor Paul Ramsey has written persuasively about the need of churches and moral critics to take seriously the dilemmas of the policymaker who because he is on the spot has some claims to be in the know. Ramsey has been influenced by the speech by Dean Acheson from which we have quoted. He believes that the church does have a responsibility to teach about presuppositions, goals, and perspectives that are the context of policy. But he says that "the church's business is not policy-formation." That is correct. And then he adds: "That is the awesome responsibility of magistrates (and of churchmen along with other citizens in their non-ecclesiastical capacities)." That is also correct. But at a later point he says that churches "need to stand in awe before people called 'decision-makers,' or rather before the majesty of the topmost political agency."[7] Here we think that he confuses the awesome nature of some decisions with the awesome nature of the decision-makers. Churches and moralists should give considerable leeway to people on the spot who are deeply involved in a concrete situation. But it is still possible for the critic who knows less about the details of the immediate situation to see how what is being done by policymakers belongs to a history of disaster. The policymaker may not see this, or may not be able to extricate himself from the consequences of his own past decisions, and may be carried along by the many pressures that surround him.

A fascinating episode during the Indochina war is recalled by Townsend Hoopes, Undersecretary of the Air Force from 1967 to 1969. In his book entitled *The Limits of Intervention,*[8] he tells of a conversation with John T. McNaughton, who was Assistant Secretary of Defense and one of Secretary McNamara's most influential advisers. "Punctilious in his public support of the Administration and personally devoted to McNamara who, he felt, was now earnestly trying to guide the war toward de-escalation and settlement (albeit within the strictures of a highly personal conception of loyalty to the President), McNaughton was by the spring of 1967 appalled by the catastrophic loss of proportion that had overtaken the U.S. military effort in Vietnam. 'We seem to be proceeding,' he said to me in barbed tones, after returning from a particular White House session, 'on the assumption that the way to eradicate Viet Cong is to destroy all the village structures, defoliate all the jungles, and then cover the entire surface of Vietnam with asphalt.' "[9] What a revelation of the predicament of a policymaker who is caught with the results of past decisions and who is governed by loyalty to his immediate superior who is governed by loyalty to *his* superior!

There is evidence that McNamara, who was one of the chief architects of the whole policy and who had done a great deal to sell it to the American people, was disillusioned about it also. These men might have made a clean break, but loyalty kept them from doing it. Think what effect it would have had upon the country if these inner thoughts of the persons so close to the "topmost political agency" had been made known to the public. Public opinion might have caught up with reality more quickly.

There is another reason for caution in accepting the authority of policymakers. It is that they are not only silent about their own questions concerning their policies but sometimes they deceive the people about the facts. They even deceive Congress. There were many instances of this during the Indochina war having to do with operations in Laos, the bombing of Cambodia, and the events in the Tonkin Gulf. The last was a matter of crucial importance because if Congress had known the facts about what happened in the Tonkin Gulf as they were later revealed in the Pentagon Papers,[10] the Tonkin Gulf resolution which formed the justification for the Administration's war policy might never have been passed by Congress. This experience must cause churches and citizens generally to seek information about the facts connected with policy. Congress cannot make policy because it is a large body not equipped for quick action. But it can do a great deal to ferret out the facts and make them available. Churches can prod Congress to do this, and in some cases their international presence may enable them to have independent sources of facts or of interpretations of facts.

We have been dealing with the decision-making of those responsible for policy. Many of them in this country are Christians whose values and sensitivities are shaped in part by Christian teaching and by their own religious commitment. This is a complicated matter because people who are sincere in their Christian profession often have ways of keeping their faith and their judgments about foreign policy in separate compartments. The same pattern is common in other fields of activity. They may also derive from their Christian background one or two ideas related to policy that may be one-sided. For example, there are persons who have a great deal of piety as Christians who assume that because Communists are antireligious, Christians should be governed in their view of international relations chiefly by anti-Communism. Also, the idea that freedom deserves a higher place than other values causes some Christians to develop a religiously supported Americanism that distorts their view of other countries which, because of different histories and needs, have had different priorities. Membership in a church that is aware of its participation in the worldwide Christian community should provide correctives for these distortions. Too often this does not happen.

Christians who try to avoid compartmentalization, who are aware of the misleading character of these distortions, and whose insight frees them from narrowly nationalistic pressures have an important contribution to make when they are in positions where they can influence policy. It should be evident that policymakers can combine faithfulness to the well-being of the nations for which they act as trustees and at the same time serve humanity's interest in peace and justice. There will be times of inner conflict for persons in such a role. Sometimes they may be so limited by public opinion that they cannot make a choice consistent with their own convictions. At times they may believe that the nation and the government are on the wrong road. The view of such persons from outside may make it seem that it would be better if they resigned, but the view from inside may be different. In good conscience they may believe that while they are on the spot they may still bring about some desirable changes in policy. Or if this responsibility is weighed with many others, more may be said for remaining on the job than for resigning. Doubtless many people who are uneasy about such inner conflicts remain on the job chiefly because of political ambition or the power and perquisites of office. Yet there is room for a conscientious struggle in many cases that could come out either way. As we have suggested, it is hard to believe that it would not have been better if there had been more resignations from the government over the Indochina war.

Moral Absolutes and Political Complexities

Many thoughtful and sensitive Christians who have no responsibility for policy form judgments on international issues on the basis of absolutistic convictions. To them some choices are in themselves wrong regardless of any calculation of consequences. Some means are so clearly evil that no calculation concerning their relation to good ends can justify resort to them. It is a commonplace of philosophical ethics to distinguish between a teleological and a deontological approach to ethics. The former refers to the tendency to emphasize the consequences of an action rather than the action in itself. The latter is the emphasis on a particular act as either good or evil because of its intrinsic nature. Those who take this deontological approach see that the act itself may be against the moral law, whatever the consequences of doing it or of refusing to do it. The person who is primarily teleological in approach may find that an act morally repellent in itself is a necessary means to an end that has a moral claim.

There will always be these two approaches to ethical

decision. In this book we try to judge acts in terms of the whole pattern of consequences that can be expected to follow from them. Yet there are situations in which a particular choice may seem dictated by a plausible calculation of consequences but which we believe to be so profoundly evil that no conceivable consequences can justify it.

Max Weber in a famous essay entitled "Politics as a Vocation"[11] makes the distinction between an "ethic of ultimate ends" and an "ethic of responsibility." These correspond to the distinction between deontological ethics and teleological ethics. It is common for those concerned about the problems of statesmanship to exalt Weber's idea of an ethic of responsibility. Weber shows his general preference when he says that those guided by the ethic of ultimate ends are more concerned about "the flame of good intentions" than about the consequences of their choices with which they and their nations will have to live. He contrasts the two types of ethics by saying that the Christian who follows the ethic of ultimate ends "does rightly and leaves the results to the Lord"; "conduct that follows the maxim of an ethic of responsibility" has to "give account of the foreseeable results of one's action."

We believe that the ethic of responsibility that involves concern for foreseeable results is usually the right approach in public issues which affect the lives and well-being of nations. To separate a particular act from the whole context of its results is artificial, for those results need to be seen as extensions of the act and they give to it part of its moral meaning. It may be more defensible to stress the particular act and say yes or no to it regardless of the results if the person who makes the choice can absorb most of those results in his or her own experience. When a continuing community has to absorb them over an indefinite period it is less defensible to run risks with them.

Yet there may be occasions where a line must be drawn against a particular act apart from calculating the results because the enormity of the evil in it may be much clearer than any such calculations. There is a relation to consequences when those who take this position argue that the means which they reject would distort or corrupt the end. Even Weber in spite of his preference for an ethic of responsibility admits that there may not be an absolute contrast between the two. At some point, he says, a person who follows the ethic of responsibility may have to stop and say of a particular choice "Here I stand; I can do no other." One may act so because of an intense intuitive conviction at the moment. But this is likely to be supported by previous human experience of the consequences of such acts as the one to which they say no.

The example of an absolutistic approach to ethics which is most relevant to our discussion of foreign policy is the ethic of absolute pacifism. The use of lethal force or violence is ruled out whatever calculations may be made about the results of using or not using them. Here we are concerned only with that form of absolute pacifism that goes beyond a vocational renunciation of such force or violence and advocates that the policy of the nation should be based on the renunciation of violence. There may be some debate in detail as to what exactly constitutes the morally forbidden violence. The word "lethal" may cover it. The use of force may be acceptable to restrain people who are injuring themselves or others, if it stops short of killing or intentional serious injury. The use of force in order to deter or to stop a riot which is not intended to kill or injure but which in an emergency may do so is on the borderline. The use of an international peacekeeping force which is allowed to use force in self-defense may be on the borderline for some pacifists.

In another chapter we shall discuss more fully the

issues raised by absolute pacifism. Its presence in a church or a nation may contribute a great deal to the atmosphere in which solutions may be found, even though it may not have the solution. Here we make two points briefly, regarding the claims of absolute pacifism to be a self-sufficient answer. The first is that a government responsible to a nation that does not have a majority of pacifists cannot in faithfulness to its special role as trustee for that nation base its policies on absolute pacifism. The other point is that in the world as it is a nation that renounces the means of self-defense makes itself unnecessarily vulnerable to aggressive power however malevolent that power may be. Though some readers may disagree with that statement, there is enough to be said for it to make absolute pacifism morally problematic as a basis for national policy. It is so politically nonviable in the United States that even pacifists should be able to consider second-best policies. When we say that it is politically nonviable in the United States, it should be pointed out that the same is true of most, if not all, other countries. Some countries may be nonmilitary but they depend on other nations to protect them in their own interests. India had more preparation to become pacifist than any other great nation, but events have proved that it is like other nations in justifying the use of military force under some conditions.

Having made these comments about the most relevant example of absolutistic thinking, we return to the point that we find places where we must draw the line. We must say no regardless of any calculation of results available to us.

One illustration is enough: There is nothing that can justify the indiscriminate bombing of populations. These include chiefly noncombatants. Even if most of the adult population are involved in some work that helps the war effort, whether they choose to be so involved or not, the children and the elderly should be regarded as benign hostages whose presence keeps a population off limits. In the Second World War both sides engaged in the saturation bombing of cities. This was also done by Americans in the bombing of large areas in Indochina though in the early stages of that war American authorities claimed that their policy was to engage only in precision bombing directed toward military targets. Both German and Japanese cities were indiscriminately bombed before the use of atomic bombs on Hiroshima and Nagasaki. Not only was the latter a clear case of indiscriminate bombing of populations; it was also the fateful inauguration of the nuclear age, with the United States setting the example for all time of *first use* of a nuclear bomb without warning. We regret that in the calculations concerning the use of the bomb on those Japanese cities, the principle of avoiding the direct bombing of populations was not even given great weight. It was lost in a pragmatic cost-benefit calculation. Moral reasoning should include particular considerations prior to all calculations of consequences which are in themselves flags of warning. Some warnings may do no more than put a heavy burden of proof on those who choose to go against them but this can be of great importance. *Others should decisively say: Stop. No thoroughfare.*

In an earlier chapter we quoted from an article by George Kennan in which he spoke of his moral rejection of the obliteration bombing of cities in the Second World War. He continued his discussion of the implications of that judgment in the following passage: "It will be said to me: This means defeat. To this I can only reply: I am skeptical of the meaning of 'victory' and 'defeat' in their relation to modern war between great countries. To my mind the defeat is war itself. In any case it seems to me that there are times when we have no choice but to follow the dictates of conscience, to throw ourselves on God's mercy, and not to ask too many questions."[12] This is moving testimony from a Christian who is both an expert and one who has been close to policymaking.

4

Morality
and National Interest

IT IS GENERALLY ASSUMED that statesmen will make the national interest their major criterion for foreign policy decisions. Governments are trustees for the nation, and it goes without saying that they do have responsibility for its interests. How ambiguous a concept national interest is! How complicated is its relation to morality! This is especially true of Christian understandings of morality. And what is true of Christian morality is also true of a more broadly based humanistic and universal morality.

National interest takes many different forms. At one end of a continuum it is preoccupation with narrow, egoistic national goals, short-run goals involving a limited and materialistic range of values. At the other end national interest can be defined in terms of long-range goals and inclusive values that express the desire of people in a nation to live in a peaceful and more just global environment. Such interests reflect awareness that all nations are bound together in a common fate. Here Christians and churches should have an important role. In their commitments and caring they should be able to identify with the well-being of people in other nations as much as with their own. In their vision they should transcend even enlightened views of national interest because they see the whole world as loved of God who has no favorites among nations. Unless there be many such people in a nation, there is much less chance that public opinion in general and the nation in its policies will move far in this continuum toward a wise and broad view of national interest.

There are some obvious ingredients of national interest. For example, it includes the security of a nation against its destruction or domination by another power or group of powers. It includes its survival as a community. It includes the well-being of its people with emphasis on their economic welfare, which involves well-functioning economic institutions. It includes safeguarding its natural environment. Yet, even on such obvious matters there can be great differences of opinion as to what best serves the nation's security or the well-being of its people. National security may not be well served by policies that have as their main purpose keeping ahead in the arms race. There is no national security except through the prevention of nuclear war. This depends more on better mutual relations between governments and peoples than it does on the building up the national military establishment. We do not believe in unilateral disarmament. We recognize that military defense has a necessary place in protecting the national interests. But usually those who put major stress on national security give it a disproportionate place.

National interest is relative to the national purpose or purposes. These include security and well-being. They also involve great emphasis on liberty. They should involve much greater emphasis on both the liberty of all classes among the people in their everyday life and on justice in their relationships. It is a commonplace that the United States, which was established as a nation by the deliberate acts of its founders, is more explicitly committed to ideals than is usually the case with nations. The historian Sidney E. Mead has written a book with a title which he took from a description of the United States by G. K. Chesterton: *The Nation with the Soul of a Church* (Harper & Row, Publishers, Inc., 1975). There is great danger in that idea, and this seems to be fully appreciated today. It has been the background of our national moral pretensions; our belief in a unique national virtue that has been much emphasized in the rhetoric of presidents. It has made it possible for President Ford to say that "America is morally and spiritually number one and that will be the force to keep us moving so that America, and all its people, its government, will be number one forever."[1]

Such self-righteous statements are offensive. But there is an important truth in the claim that our country was founded on ideals in spite of all the contrasts between those ideals and its behavior. The "self-evident" truth "that all men are created equal, that they are endowed by their Creator with certain unalienable Rights, that among these are Life, Liberty, and the pursuit of Happiness" sets forth an ideal of equality in stark contrast with the reality of slavery when the great Declaration was signed. It remains in stark contrast with the poverty of about twenty-six million of our people today, especially those who belong to racial minorities. It was taken for granted during most of our history that justice would be realized as a by-product of seeking liberty for all. We know from bitter experience that this is an error.

Yet, with all that can be said in criticism of our one-sided national idealism and of the contrast between our ideals and the reality of our national life, national interest must include service to the national purpose which includes the ideal of human rights, so well expressed in the Bill of Rights. Our best leaders have never thought of imposing our ideals by force on other nations. There has been, however, an American messianism that did not shrink from this, especially when it became joined with the idea of America as the nation whose duty it was to save parts of the world from Communism. Anything seemed to be justified including the bombing of populations and the assassination of heads of states when we sought ways to curb or undercut Communist nations. All of this has backfired. If it once seemed justified as a method of serving a national purpose, today it can be seen to be wrong in itself and self-defeating so far as our purpose is concerned. It has caused our ideals to be associated in many places with capitalistic imperialism and with a cruel aggressiveness in American policy and strategy.

We serve our ideals best when we are more humble; when we abandon the self-righteous pose that has been a blight on our role in the world; when we identify with the human rights of people in nations on the political right as much as in nations on the political left; when we show a greater concern to help people to be delivered from injustice, from poverty and hunger. Service to these ideals abroad will be helped if there can be a more adequate embodiment of them in our own national life. All of this will be in the national interest in a real sense.

In line with the best in our idealism is the breaking down of the barriers between peoples so that our people may share in the life of a universal human community. This is doubtless implied in the goal set forth by Dean Acheson concerning the flourishing of free societies, for free societies are open to one another. One tragic aspect of the attempts of some governments to limit emigration and to control what people read or hear is that it deprives the people of the chance to participate in this larger community. It also deprives the people of other nations of enriching relations with their own people. Some barriers have been partly broken down but this goal is still far away. We should seek it as a great good in itself, as a part of the fulfillment of the humanity of our own people, and in their own national interest.

We have emphasized in Chapter 1 the constructive role of national interest in contrast to ideological or idealistic crusading. This kind of crusading often knows no limits and it may be terribly destructive. When the emphasis is focused on real and tangible national interests, a nation's use of power may be more readily restrained than when it serves ideals that express a one-sided American ideology. National interest as a source of national restraint may actually lead to more constructive moral achievement than moralistic crusading. The same thing is true of nations governed by Marxist ideology. It is good news when they become concerned about the well-being of their own people and are not engaged in fomenting revolution ten thousand miles away.

In what follows we shall discuss national interest under two aspects: (1) national interest as part of a more inclusive human interest, and (2) the ambiguity of national interest seen in the wide spectrum of views concerning what constitutes national interest.

So long as national interest includes the well-being of all the people in one's nation, the well-being of two hundred and fifteen million Americans or of eight and a half million Cubans, that interest is part of the common interest of humanity as a whole. That means the whole population and not only the thin layer on top which is often what governments have in mind. It is no small thing to do what we can to serve it. When real conflicts of interest arise between two or more nations, policymakers should understand that their opposite numbers in the other countries have the same responsibilities as trustees for their nations as they have for their own. This should help to prepare the way for decent accommodations of interests. One thing that wise policymakers have learned is that it is essential to help their opposite numbers and the nations they represent to save face when they make concessions. Even beyond that, in a world in which large-scale poverty anywhere contributes to a destructive instability everywhere, it becomes important to our national interest to do what we can to help other nations realize their interest in a better life for their poor.

This is the picture of international relations for which we may hope. Often the reality is quite different because instead of acting as trustees for the well-being of their people, governments are moved by old hostilities, by vested interests in a policy that makes them resist change, by living within a vicious circle of fear, by ideologies that distort their estimate of the real interests of all concerned, by identification of the national interest with the interests of particular economic groups in their own country that are operating abroad, or by dreams of power and glory that may have nothing to do with the well-being of anyone. Insofar as we can free our concept of national interest from such perversions, it has an important though limited moral claim as a guide for national policy.

Our chief concern is to develop what has been said about the wide spectrum of views held regarding national interest. It is sufficient for our purpose to discuss views that are common in the United States. At one extreme there are those who are strongly nationalistic, who have little interest in the welfare of other countries, who often put great emphasis on this nation's being *first* in power and in wealth. They have few questions about the rightness of what their country has done in the world. They are preoccupied with ideological differences between the United States and nations that are influenced to any degree by Marxism or even by democratic socialism. Whenever their country acts abroad they prefer to have it do so unilaterally. Their chief trust so far as national security is concerned is in military strength. Nationalists of this type are edgy about possible threats from other nations, whether those nations are as weak as Panama or as powerful as the Soviet Union. This leads them to identify national interest largely with national power to meet remotely possible threats. They have no patience with multilateral institutions that may in any way limit national sovereignty. For them the United Nations is especially offensive because the United States no longer controls a majority of its members.

This is a familiar pattern. While those various tendencies often go together, such a consistently narrow nationalism is a minority view, though elements of it under the stimulus of provocative events do gain widespread popularity. The sudden rise in President Ford's popularity following the Mayaguez affair may be mentioned as an example. Professor Seyom Brown cites impressive evidence to show that even after the frustrations of the Indochina war American opinion remained basically internationalist and even altruistic. The American idealism which can take the form of self-righteous crusading can also represent a genuine concern for the well-being of people in other countries. Professor Brown refers to polls taken in 1972 and recorded by Watts and Free in *State of the Nation*. Sixty-three percent of the population agreed with the proposition: "The United States should cooperate fully with the United Nations." This result was down only 9 percentage points since 1964 in spite of the apparent disillusionment with the United Nations. More important are the results of surveys conducted by the Overseas Development Council in 1972 which showed that "public support for the idea of assistance to underdeveloped countries is at an historic high of 68 percent." Professor Brown draws the following conclusion: "This phenomenon of persisting internationalism and altruism cannot be adequately explained without reference to the deep strain of idealism in the American political character which continually seeks universal expression. The country sees itself at its best as a place where people of all cultures, religions, and nationalities share domicile and power—a model, perhaps, for fashioning the polity of the globe."[2] After we have been well warned about all the perversions of American idealism, we should hope that it will not be smothered by the warnings!

A new factor is evident in attitudes that have been very common in recent student generations which strengthen the better side of this idealism. President Kingman Brewster of Yale University wrote an article in *Foreign Affairs* (April 1972) to show that the United States is not likely to become isolationist. He emphasized the attitudes of students whom he knew so well. He said the following about them: "The current student generation's misgivings about the universal wisdom and virtue of the American experiment clashes sharply with the self-righteous scorn for the vicissitudes of the foreigner which has always been such a large part of the isolationist tradition. Also, they are more genuinely imbued with an interest in and enthusiasm about peoples, nations, cultures other than their own than any preceding generation of Americans ever has been." That was written more than five years ago and student attitudes change quickly. Today students may be less articulate on these matters and quite naturally often more worried about jobs than anything else. But we doubt if there is among them a narrow nationalism or ideological rigidity. We doubt if they are more impressed than was the case five years ago by chauvinistic Americanism. Indeed one thing seems to be true of a great many, though today the financial limitations are greater, which President Brewster notes: "All of this is fostered by the fantastic ease with which they wander.

To many of them nothing is strange."

These attitudes are in line with the international out-look which we find at the other end of the spectrum of interpretations of the national interest. Those represented here would see American interest as best served by having a peaceful world, by defusing conflicts—including ideological conflicts with other nations—by participating in real concessions and even sacrifices in plans that help other nations to overcome poverty and hunger. It is not in our national interest to be a prosperous oasis in a world of misery. This is true in part because we have a stake in mutually advantageous economic relations with other countries. We also have a stake in what is often called stability. But this need not mean the preservation of the *status quo* against revolutionary change, but rather the desire to prevent continuous tumult or anarchy which benefits no one. The violence of despairing people, of which the political hijacking of airplanes is an example, represents the destructive instability which is not in our interests. It calls attention, however, to problems for which we should seek solutions in our own interest. This view of national interest would involve a willingness to limit sovereignty through participation in multilateral institutions to prevent war and to deal with the global economic and environmental problems that affect the welfare of the whole world.

We have said enough to indicate how far the concept of national interest can be stretched without abandoning it. There are real conflicts of interest among nations. One of the most spectacular is the conflict over oil between the nations that produce most of it and those which are the greatest consumers. This is not an absolute conflict in the long run because the bankruptcy of the consumers would deprive the producers of an essential market. Nations do have to look to their own economic interest. Conflicts over access to resources are likely to be acute, but it should be an axiom that there is no military solution to such conflicts. Military action to gain control of resources in Third World countries would stir up resentment on an enormous scale against those who took such action. There is surprising power in the resentment of large blocs of deprived nations, generally former victims of colonialism, against new forms of Western colonialism.

Many cases of economic conflict today are between nations that have a stake in each other's well-being. For example, particular forms of economic competition between the United States and Japan, between the United States and West Germany, or between the United States and Canada do not annul the American interest in the economic health and political viability of all three nations. We see on the horizon conflicts of interest growing out of the immigration policies of rich countries in relation to the enormous increase of population in poor countries. We doubt if anyone is prepared morally or intellectually to deal with that type of conflict as it becomes more acute.

In such situations an ethic of prudential mutuality breaks down. A policy that keeps others alive will not keep us alive and vice versa. When there is not enough arable land for the world's population, or enough oil or its substitutes for the world's energy needs, then our common interests, even our common interest in peace, may easily be subordinated to a selfish interest in having our next meals come to us. Can we imagine a more soul-destroying prospect than an elemental violent struggle for existence between peoples growing out of shortages of food and energy?

If this is the prospect that lies ahead for the world, the contribution of those whose empathy and outgoing love for people of other nations that takes them beyond even an enlightened view of national interest will be crucial. They should help the nation as a whole to move to a new level of perceptions and concerns. It must be a level which recognizes that it is in the interest of the people of a nation to retain their full humanity, to be able to live with their consciences without shame or a searing sense of guilt. It is not in the American interest to survive meanly in a world of death. A glimpse of such possibilities in time may push a nation, which is always inclined to postpone difficult decisions, to use its brains and its resources to find new and unexpected solutions to problems; to find new ways of life in which there is hope for humanity.

As Professor Joseph S. Nye puts it: "The rapid rise in population and likely inability of South Asians to grow enough food to avert famine may appear as a South Asian problem from which we can isolate ourselves if we consider it in purely physical terms. It is highly likely, however, in an age of modern satellite communications that many Americans will demand a major U.S. policy response after watching people starve on the evening news before sitting down to ample dinners. The new items on the agenda will affect even the staunchest neo-isolationist who never sets foot outside our borders and professes to care little about the rest of the world."[3]

We cite two American leaders: one, a statesman, and the other, the most influential journalist of the past generation, as they have reflected on this relation of conscience to national interest. Both have always stressed the responsibility of the government as the trustee for national interest. Both have used national interest as a check upon grandiose uses of national power. Both men were discussing the grounds for foreign economic aid by the United States to other countries.

Senator James W. Fulbright in 1965 wrote the following: "The continuing need of the rich countries to assist poor countries is a matter of both political and moral compulsion. It is difficult to see how the world's less developed countries can overcome their enormous social and economic problems without generous assistance from the more favored nations, and it is difficult to see how the rich countries can expect to be secure in their affluence as islands in a global sea of misery. But beyond the social and economic and political and strategic reasons for the rich aiding the poor is the simple motive of humanitarian conscience."[4]

It should be said about that statement that such aid should not be given with emphasis upon our generosity or in expectation of gratitude. On the other hand it should not be given as though it was done only in our own interests, because then the receiving nations may feel that they are being used. On this delicate matter it is difficult to win, whatever one says or does. But awareness of both dangers may at least help our representatives to avoid great and gauche errors. There should be an effort to stretch the idea of mutual interest as far as it can go even though one may go beyond it.

The journalist to whom I refer is Walter Lippmann, who made a specialty of foreign policy. He was noted for what we may call a wise realism and for the independence of his mind. In 1963 he wrote the following about motives for foreign aid: "The poor wretches who have to sell foreign aid to Congress have been taught that they are advocates of an act of unnatural generosity. The cardinal rule is that they must avoid the suspicion that our motives in giving foreign aid are in the smallest degree disinterested. They must hide any compassion they may have or any feeling that the powerful and the rich have obligations to the weak and the poor. The accepted way to get the money voted is for the President to cross his heart and swear that every dollar will be used to hire allies and to confound our adversaries." He concludes his discussion by saying that "it is the duty, not merely the national interest, of all nations, rich and poor alike, to provide the funds to finance world development."[5]

We may want to find a better word than "aid" which has paternalistic overtones. Also, the word "development" is resisted in many circles, especially in Latin America, as suggesting something which belongs to the agenda of the so-called "developed nations." But both Fulbright and Lippmann dealt with the mixture of motives that will be present in relations between privileged and disadvantaged nations, whatever words may be used. Both men broke out of the limits set by an egoistic view of national interest.

We are convinced that both men spoke for a majority of the American people, but presidents and legislators are sensitive to the pressures of well-organized minorities. For this reason our policies often fail to do justice to the feelings of most Americans.

Stretch the conception of national interest as we may, there will usually be tension between the perspectives of the church and those of persons responsible for national policy. The reason is that the latter begin with their responsibilities for their own country. This is where they start, though they may be sensitive to the claims of the largest view of the national interest. The church starts as a universal community, and then what is valid in national interests finds its place within the larger vision. We realize that this may seem an ideal picture of the church, but the more churches within a nation—even the local congregations—are true to their essential nature, the more likely it will be that the nation will be influenced by that larger vision. Contrast and even tension between church and state in this context are good for both. Expressions of such tension are favored by the religious freedom that is part of our national heritage.

We would carry that last point a step further. It is part

of our country's tradition that it should be open to a higher law above the state and to a universal good beyond the good of the nation. The language was that of another day, but it is significant that James Madison, who as much as anyone was responsible for the U.S. Constitution, wrote: "Before any man can be considered a member of civil society, he must be considered as a subject of the governor of the universe." Abraham Lincoln, amid the trying events of his time, most movingly expressed his faith by submitting his nation and his cause to "the judgments of the Lord" which are "true and righteous altogether." And in a more recent time the U.S. Supreme Court said in the words of Justice William O. Douglas: "The victory for freedom of thought recorded in our Bill of Rights recognizes that in the domain of conscience there is a moral power higher than the state." (Girourd Case, 1946.) May we not say that on the moral problems in international relations the finest sensitivities of the national conscience receive support not only from the churches but also from that openness in the American tradition to judgment from above the nation?

5

Personal Options
and Modern War

IN ADDITION to the policies of nations with respect to war, decisions must be made by individuals regarding their own participation in or support of war. This is one of the most excruciatingly difficult choices faced by thoughtful persons. Especially is this true with the more widespread and devastating evil consequences of modern war on the one hand and the greater propaganda and conscripting power of modern governments on the other hand. Furthermore, more persons are confronted with this choice as entire populations are increasingly involved in a major war effort. Working in plants producing the weapons for mechanized warfare may be as direct a support of killing as is army service in a more detached assignment behind the lines.

In speaking of the difficulty of a decision about Christian duty in wartime, Augustine said, "Let everyone, then, who thinks with pain on all these great evils, so horrible, so ruthless, acknowledge that this is misery. And if anyone either endures or thinks of them without mental pain, this is a more miserable plight still, for he thinks himself happy because he has lost human feeling."[1]

Three positions have been prominent in the history of Christian attitudes toward war.[2] One of these can quickly be dismissed in the light of modern ethical sensitivity. The view of the "holy war" or "crusade" has become anachronistic on both theological and sociological grounds. As illustrated in the Old Testament and in many of the religious wars of later history, this view regards a particular war as waged in an overwhelmingly righteous cause, attempting to destroy what is clearly a gross evil. The First World War was so regarded even by many prominent religious leaders. Enlistment is so enthusiastic in such a war that one might appropriately feel, as in the Crusades, that Christ was leading the hosts of the Lord to battle and that by participation one would win the reward of salvation. No valid conscientious objection to such a war would be recognized. There is no sense of tragedy or of involvement in evil. To use phrases from Max Stackhouse, since there is no "critical distance" from the war, it is likely to be accompanied by a "frenzy of wrath" or even "orgies of devastation."[3]

Persons committed to peace as a goal and informed about the ambiguities of modern international relationship can no longer accept such a view of war. Even when they vigorously wage a particular war, they cannot regard it as a crusade. The Second World War was less regarded as a crusade than as a necessary evil. It is theologically impossible to involve God in war to such an extent as to exorcise all evil out of the hostilities. If the concept of war as crusade is set aside, this leaves two general positions to be considered. A conscientious person then chooses some variation of either the just-war theory or the pacifist position. Either the Christian will regard war as possibly a necessary evil (or the best possible choice under the existing circumstances), or he or she will refuse to participate in war.

CURRENT RELEVANCE OF TRADITIONAL JUST WAR THEORY

Except for the strong pacifist tendencies of the early church, the doctrine of the just war has been the predominant approach of the Christian tradition. According to this approach, war was considered an evil, though participation was permitted in those wars which met certain criteria. These standards were variously listed, but have come to include the following major tests:

1. A justifiable war is one waged by a legitimate sovereign rather than by individuals or unauthorized groups.

2. War is to be undertaken as a last resort, only after all other superior means have been exhausted.

3. Motivation is the intention to advance important good or to avoid grievous evil, rather than less just motives like greed or vengeance.

4. According to the principle of proportionality, a just war must accomplish more good than harm.

5. There must be a reasonable hope of success in achieving right ends. A nation should not sacrifice its sons and daughters or decimate other peoples and countries when there is little probability of achieving right ends.

6. Any war to be just must be fought with humane means. It must be conducted with sufficient moderation, for example, to protect the rights of civilians and prisoners. In this connection, along with the principle of proportionality, Paul Ramsey has insisted on noncombatant immunity as an essential part of traditional doctrine. Civilians are not to be directly attacked even though there is the double effect of secondary unintended casualties among civilians.[4]

In the light of considerations that have recently become more obvious, additional questions need to be added to those traditionally raised by the doctrine of the just war. In a day in which we are increasingly conscious of ecological costs, the consequences of war must also be measured in terms of scarce materials and of advanced pollution. One must also assess the extent to which an appeal to might to determine right increases power for the already powerful, and perhaps wealth for the already wealthy. In proportionately balancing gains and losses, less weight is to be given to the protection or enhancement of the material goods of wealthy nations now that we see the necessity for lowering their material standards of living. Another major question is the impact of any war on the poor of the earth. In reference to the Mekong Delta Project with its potential for feeding the hungry in Southeast Asia, Lester B. Pearson said, "It would make the angels weep to think that less than one-third of the money that has been spent in one year by the United States in the prosecution of the Vietnam war would complete this wonderfully imaginative project."[5]

Some have rejected outright these criteria for a just war either as anachronistic or because they have almost never been applied to the wars of one's own nation. Yet this approach is not obsolete. It was used by numerous persons in the case of the Vietnam war. Such criteria of justice become more important than ever as the international dilemmas which confront us become more complex. The question before us is not the relevance of just war theory, but rather whether, on the basis of these guidelines, one can still find a war which is justifiable.

It is clear that a major nuclear war unleashing all our weaponry could not be justified by any end that might possibly be achieved. Such a war would violate the criteria of proportionality, hope of success, and just means. Vatican II was emphatic in saying: "Any act of war aimed indiscriminately at the destruction of entire cities or of extensive areas along with their population is a crime against God and man himself. It merits unequivocal and unhesitating condemnation."[6] Full-scale modern warfare involves such evil means as to distort any worthwhile end to the point of becoming unrecognizable. In attempting to defend the state, such a war destroys the state. Instead of gaining freedom or justice through such a war we are likely to reap dictatorship and injustice. Such a "protection" of moral values makes us more callous about moral standards. There is no reasonable hope for victory, because such a war cannot be won.

Since wars involving the vital interests of great powers are almost certain to escalate, even a limited war in that category becomes suspect. Very few modern wars can be conducted with the moderation demanded by classical guidelines. It has also been argued that for purposes of waging war in our existing highly interdependent world, single nation-states are no longer legitimate sovereigns in the sense of traditional just war theory. While this argument anticipates international structures not yet available, it nevertheless raises a basic issue we must soon face. At what point does it become unjust for any nation to take justice into its own hands by waging war as an instrument of national policy? This is a particularly crucial question when so many other nations not directly involved also suffer calamitous consequences.

The requirement that a just war must be a measure of last resort would assume that combatants had exhausted all possible approaches of first resort. We now have more alternatives to war than were once available. We have a greater understanding of psychological processes and international dynamics, and a longer experience with options available through the United Nations. It would seem that war is not now justifiable unless first-resort alternatives have been thoroughly explored. Have we imaginatively used diplomacy in a problem-solving approach that genuinely takes into account the interests of the other side? Have we consistently supported international organizations sufficiently to establish their prestige and authority? Have we sacrificially supported economic development and new international forms of economic justice? Have we as far as possible dealt with the basic economic and political causes of war?

A REALISTIC VIEW OF THE PACIFIST POSITION

The same objections that seriously question the justifiability of much modern war constitute an argument for pacifism, or refusal to participate in war. Before we evaluate this position, it is important to recognize several types of pacifism, since they are not all subject to the same criticism. One may draw the line of personal objection to war at different points. Or different persons may object for different reasons. Furthermore pacifists, like nonpacifists, are not always entirely consistent. The result is a variety of individualized positions which can be roughly grouped. The absolute pacifist, who believes that the only acceptable position is complete noncooperation with all wars, has already been discussed. There are selective conscientious objectors, who make their decisions on the basis of the characteristics of each situation and who refuse to participate in particular wars that do not meet their accepted criteria. One variety of selective pacifist is the nuclear pacifist, who feels that any war involving the use of nuclear weapons, at least in their strategic form, forfeits any claim to conscientious support. They may also reject the use of tactical nuclear weapons because their use crosses the nuclear threshold or firebreak.

Also to be distinguished are the vocational pacifists. In the present situation they do not advocate their more thoroughgoing position for all persons or for governments. They do see the need for some witnesses to maintain a strong testimony in order that national policy will move closer to the ultimate goal than would otherwise be the case. Perhaps because of their particular position in the structure of society, they feel an individual call-ing in the direction of an absolute pacifist witness. At the same time they recognize that others may be called to a different creative expression. A parallel illustration might be drawn from the area of penal reform. Among those who want fundamentally to alter the present prison system, some will accept the vocation of prison warden in order to improve present arrangements and to maintain whatever protections prisons give society until something better can be built. Other persons in a more dramatic witness to public opinion may refuse to become prison wardens. Under most circumstances both groups are needed for maximum acceleration of social change.

There are strong arguments for the pacifist approach. It is increasingly difficult to justify modern war. The tendency of war is to be self-defeating. There are other important alternatives frequently available to us. Non-violent resistance, for example, under the leadership of Gandhi won independence from colonialism, and has had notable successes in other conflict situations. Con-scientious citizens, searching for a more productive method for the nation, should be considered among our most loyal and creative citizens. The spirit of love, which is at the heart of the way of Jesus, points us in the direction of nonviolence. All these considerations sug-gest that the person who has never seriously considered the pacifist position is not sufficiently sensitive to ethi-cal and religious values.

Another form of insensitivity characterizes those who uncritically and simplistically accept the pacifist posi-tion. There are other values than peace to be actualized. One can become a thoughtful pacifist only after looking at the arguments on the other side. These arguments are based on the recognition that in an imperfect world the best we can possibly do is to approximate our ultimate goals. The evil actions of others limit the alternatives available to us. It is repeatedly necessary to settle for less of one value for the sake of gaining more of another. Such trade-offs frequently have to be made, for example, between productivity and leisure, freedom and order, or peace and justice.

The arguments to be faced by the pacifist, especially of the absolutist type, reflect certain stubborn realities of the present world. At this point in history to renounce in advance all use of military force under all future imaginable and unimaginable circumstances leaves a nation exposed to destruction or domination by an aggressive and oppressive power. We doubt the moral justification of such a policy. Let it be granted that there are nonviolent methods of resistance that are inadequately explored. These should be explored and preparations made for their use. Until new discoveries are made in developing such methods, we cannot assume that they will be adequate to all circumstances. Are there not totalitarian forms of power and technological forms of aggression against which they would have little effect? It is hard to see how a resister on the ground could influence a bombardier in the air or the government that has just sent a nuclear missile on its way. While nonviolent methods can undoubtedly have a certain power against invading or occupying forces, even this requires a population well disciplined and trained in the essential tactics. Given the present positions of existing populations, nonviolent resistance is scarcely an adequate method for all immediate purposes.

Defense against aggression, especially when aggression means imposing a tyranny by one nation on another, has a very strong claim to moral justification. The current pattern of nuclear deterrence cannot be the final answer to the problem of security against nuclear attack. But as things are today, we doubt if it would be right to advocate policies that would lead to a decisive monopoly of nuclear power in any one nation or in any one alliance of nations. Time is definitely running out for the kind of military measures on which we have relied in the past. At the same time pacifism in its more simplistic forms is not a self-sufficient answer to the problems of national security and international conflict. Responsible pacifists can make a major contribution to a more peaceful world. It would be well if the numbers of the more politically astute pacifists were multiplied. At the same time, in the chapters to follow, we will need to present a more complex and comprehensive program for building the foundations of peace.

GROWING AGREEMENT BETWEEN PACIFIST AND JUST WAR APPROACHES

In the two preceding sections we have discussed the possibilities of a more radical application of just war theory and the necessity for a realistic approach to pacifism. These two trends have produced a greater convergence between the two general viewpoints. There are still important differences in substance and in emphasis, but among larger numbers of persons there is a wider area of agreement on matters like the following:

1. A distinction must be made between personal witness and public policy. For example, a militant partisan convinced of the justice of an obscure cause should not expect his country to declare a war which the majority oppose. Likewise, pacifists may act out their personal convictions and may agitate for a radical national policy, but they cannot expect their government to impose a pacifist policy on a nonpacifist electorate. There is no political possibility in the foreseeable future that the United States will have a pacifist majority or that any candidate for high national office could be elected on a pacifist platform.

In this situation persons committed to a more distant

goal also have an obligation to give attention to next steps toward that goal which can be democratically taken by their nation. Citizens still act with integrity when they personally refuse to work in an arms plant, but also vote for a candidate who, while supporting arms appropriations, has a better overall position on foreign policy than his or her opponent. Even if they feel the pacifist position to be the ideal one, policymakers and citizens who want their influence to count in the development of the best viable policy still have to think in terms of a second-best alternative. If by insisting on perfection we actually make improvement less likely and throw elections to the nationalists and chauvinists, the consequences become disastrous.

2. There is now widespread agreement among thoughtful persons that a pacifist witness should be kept alive as a steady stimulus to the rest of the population. We should acknowledge with gratitude the important positive role of pacifist minorities. Pacifists can modify the tendency of a nation to resort thoughtlessly to military force or to overrespond to provocative events in a belligerent spirit. (We might think of this belligerent spirit as a Mayaguez complex!) Pacifists often have eyes to see sooner than others what is wrong in the national posture. They have institutions, like the American Friends Service Committee, ready to act in humanitarian response to emergencies. By their full concentration on a single issue they often recognize more clearly the forces in national life that lead to an overemphasis on military power. Perhaps most important of all, they have the incentive to explore the possibilities in nonviolent resolutions of conflicts and nonviolent resistance to oppressive powers, and to keep this alternative before the church and the public mind.

3. There is widespread recognition of the difficulties in the absolute pacifist position. The possibility that some revolutionary violence may be necessary to unseat

the systemic violence of reactionary, repressive regimes
causes some hesitation to condemn all forms of violence. Such a judgment makes it easier also to accept
international military actions for highly desirable ends
and strictly limited as to aim, geographical extent,
weapons used, and duration. So long as we have large
areas of near anarchy or potential anarchy in the world,
and so long as we lack an international police force to
create some kind of order, might not limited national
forces, preferably under some kind of multilateral umbrella, on occasion be the only recourse?

If one believed it impossible to contain limited wars,
or if all foreseeable wars appeared too evil to support,
an absolute pacifist position might be the best option.
Yet even such a person might be situational enough in
judgment to admit that circumstances might emerge in
which a sufficiently limited war might be approved. For
such reasons, numbers of persons who call themselves
pacifists would classify themselves not as absolutists,
but perhaps as nuclear or vocational pacifists.

4. Even those who consider themselves nonpacifists
can now admit that there is a solid case for selective
pacifism (including nuclear pacifism) and for vocational pacifism. A minority of the population so situated
in the social structure that it feels itself vocationally
called by God to a more radical witness is a desirable aid
to public policy, especially if it does not claim superior
virtue for itself. But the claim of selective pacifism is
even wider than that of vocational pacifism. In principle, as we have defined selective pacifism and the just
war position, the two can become the same. So long as
selective pacifists accept criteria similar to those
adopted by the radical just war theorists, the two groups
are following the same methods and guidelines. The
just war position implies selective conscientious objection.

Differences in emphasis, available data, or conclusions become individual differences rather than group differences. All conscientious persons should now become selective pacifists or fearless just war practioners. (Take your choice of title!) At the same time, some of us are undoubtedly being called by God to become vocational pacifists with a more comprehensive conscientious objection to war.

5. We clearly need to lengthen the list of wars that cannot be considered justifiable and in which it is not appropriate for conscientious persons to participate. There is no defense and no victory in a major nuclear war. It destroys any end for which it is waged. As realistic a specialist in international relations as Hans Morgenthau concludes, "I would say without qualification that a thermonuclear war, however begun, cannot be justified on moral grounds."[7] We also need to add to the unacceptable list such wars as involve the vital interests of nuclear powers and are therefore likely to escalate into nuclear war. Under present military capabilities, both the First and Second World Wars probably could not be repeated without disaster to the whole human race. Any all-out war using the modern capabilities of conventional arms would probably come under the ban, since in the calculus of calamity, enough conventional bombs equal a nuclear bomb—not to mention chemical or biological weapons.

Another addition to the list of proscribed wars might well be ideological wars of intervention by great powers to impose their will on weaker nations. Perhaps we have also learned the uselessness of trying by military means to support unpopular governments against mass discontent among their peoples. We should recognize as immoral any military support for reactionary regimes against popularly supported movements of national liberation.

While such narrower limits to wars that we could

support would not take us all the way to absolute pacifism, it would move us toward it. For example, absolute pacifism has never been a part of official Roman Catholic teaching, but Pope John XXIII came near to it when he said, "It is hardly possible to imagine that in the atomic era war could be used as an instrument of justice."[8] The burden of proof is now on governments that engage in war, since even those who are not absolute pacifists are driven to the conclusion that any modern war is likely to be unjustifiable. The burden of proof has also shifted to those Christians who believe it appropriate to use international violence.[9]

6. A sixth point on which there is widespread agreement is the urgent necessity for more consistent and skillful use of alternatives to war. A first such alternative is a foreign policy that will both prevent the outbreak of hostilities and secure greater freedom and justice. Pacifists can make common cause with non-pacifists on such items as: working against hawkish and militaristic attitudes; overcoming the causes of war; strengthening international institutions, including the United Nations; bringing about reconciliation between peoples; renouncing the effort to establish or maintain American dominance; taming American-based multinational corporations; and moving toward constructive approaches to poverty, hunger, and international justice.

A second area for cooperative effort is the further development of the potentialities in nonviolent resistance for use in place of military methods should conflict erupt. While our present capabilities in nonviolence have limitations, there have also been enough successes for the method to demand attention. The sociological processes and theological presuppositions involved are already rather well understood.[10] To make the method even more clearly an alternative, we need further mobilization of the social sciences for research, of the mass media for public education, and of agencies like the church for changing attitudes and training in the disciplines of the method. What would happen if we poured into such enterprises only a portion of the resources we now use in research and training for war?

Christians have always claimed that there is power in love and that evil can be overcome with good. We have yet to discover the full, practical strategies through which this mighty transformation can be released into international life. All "creation waits with eager longing" for this revelation.

6

An Evaluation
of Military Deterrence

CAN IT BE that nations at the historic peak of military power are left with less international influence than ever before? If this should turn out to be the case, it would reverse a long-standing conviction still commonly accepted as axiomatic. Present national policy is based on a strong public opinion that the best prevention of war is such a buildup of military strength as will deter any aggressor. Is this fact or fallacy? A sound analysis of this popular proposition is one of the greatest prerequisites for peace. War will be prevented neither by wishing for peace nor by unquestioningly following the paths of the past.

THE NATURE OF DETERRENCE

A policy of deterrence aims at maintaining sufficient military strength that other nations will hesitate to attack. This can take the form of seeking such dominance that other nations know they have no possibility of winning their objectives through war. Secretary of Defense James Forrestal is said to have hung on his office wall, "We will never have peace until the strongest army and the strongest navy are in the hands of the world's most powerful nation." Or deterrence may take the form of such a parity of power that all antagonists involved know that any possible military victory would bring such unacceptable damage to themselves that any gain would not be worth the cost. This does not necessarily mean parity at every point. One nation might have more manpower in its armies, while another might have more planes in its air force. In nuclear days the symmetry of power would leave to major nations enough bombs to provide a balance of threatened devastation.

Deterrence is the doctrine that "one sword holds another in its sheath." Winston Churchill put it into more modern terms when he suggested that we might reach a stage "where safety will be the sturdy child of terror, and survival the twin-brother of annihilation." Or deterrence can be described as the principle in which the population and industries of another nation are held as hostages. If that nation does not remain peaceful, the hostages will be killed or destroyed. This involves a threat of retaliation sufficient to make the goal of an opponent appear unattainable or at least excessively costly. The level of threat needs to be high enough and obvious enough to deter even irrational or desparate leaders in other nations. Lest we blunder into war because of a false assessment of the situation, the realities of power must be clear enough as to make miscalculation unlikely.

The Case for Deterrence

Adequate national policy requires an analysis of both the strengths and the weaknesses of deterrence, considering arguments both for and against. A number of important arguments have been used to support this approach.

1. A policy of military deterrence takes seriously the realities of the present situation. Utopian dreaming makes no contribution if the dreamer and his friends are enslaved or annihilated. Any action that is to con-

tribute to human well-being must do so within the circumstances which actually exist. In our time nations do act in their own interests. Before embarking on military adventures national leaders do weigh gains and losses with respect to those interests. When on matters of basic or vital interest they are prepared to undertake military action, it can be argued that they understand only the language of corresponding force.

2. Our cultural context being what it is, it is argued that an effective deterrent would prevent war. It has done so historically. In the present situation modern weapons have introduced a degree of threatened loss which is especially impressive. A balance of terror has held nuclear arsenals in check. Knowing that they may be utterly destroyed by retaliation, great powers have acted cautiously in their use of military force. Nations recognize that they are better off to yield certain points than to press on into devastating war. No nation will resort to a war it is sure to lose or in which the nation will suffer unacceptable damage. The expense of our armaments is a small price to pay for so great a gain as continued peace.

3. It is hoped that deterrence will force the potential adversary to become more cooperative in practice and conciliatory in negotiations, making diplomatic agreement more likely. Any military weakness gives a diplomatic advantage to the other side which it is likely to exploit by vigorously pressing its demands. The scenario suggested by the proponents of a deterrence policy sees a buildup of our military strength followed by the backing down of our opponents from inflexible positions and negotiating more productively. This is seen to include a greater readiness to accept disarmament agreements when the cost of continuing the arms race becomes too great. Ever more destructive armaments in our arsenal are therefore seen as bargaining chips

toward disarmament. Winston Churchill claimed, "We arm to parley."

Nations have always preferred to negotiate from positions of strength. Government leaders have long thought that national political prestige and power are primarily based on military might. The prevailing definition of a "great power" is written largely in terms of a census of armaments.

4. Armed might is now especially necessary to deter nuclear blackmail. According to this argument, another nation, by simply threatening attack, could force us to accept whatever concessions it demanded. These demands might not be complete surrender, but such limited political and economic transfers of power that they would finally add up to capitulation. We would be helpless to prevent the domination of other nations over us. We would have no other way to ward off their demands. The hijacker, by threatening to kill the hostages, can force payment of a ransom so long as there is no gun trained on him.

If by unilateral disarmament we allowed a vacuum of power to develop, we would in effect encourage aggression, making war more likely. When a country is convinced that there will be no effective opposition to its action, it is powerfully tempted to move into the vacuum. Total disarmament would give a decisive advantage to any nation that developed arms secretly. Concealing a few nuclear weapons in a way that would escape detection might allow a nation to hold the rest of the world as hostage to gain its ends.

5. At least it can be argued that deterrence, while it might become self-defeating in the long run, nevertheless is the best available expedient in the immediate future. Since we do not yet have alternatives fully developed, this policy provides stopgap protection. By postponing hostilities, it allows us to buy time to build stronger foundations for more constructive interna-

tional relations. Unless we use the best available short-run policy, the explosion of major war will not allow us to stay around to work at anything in the long run. At the same time that we recognize that the actual use of our weapons in a general nuclear war would destroy all that we are trying to defend, we might accept their possession as a necessary interim strategy to create enough uncertainty about our intentions to prevent others from starting a nuclear war.

6. If these arguments are sound, then there is an ethical basis for a deterrence policy. The value-laden ends to be attained justify the means of threatening force. It is often claimed that developing military strength becomes an expression of an altruistic concern toward allies—or at least a contribution to the defense of our common interests. Nations too poor to match the expensive modern arsenals of superpowers may feel safer under our nuclear umbrella. Our preparedness then becomes a way of reassuring our friends and supporting our allies. Even more important from Biblical, theological, and humanitarian perspectives is the contribution such a policy might make to the peace of the world. According to the proponents of deterrence, preparation for war becomes a way to peace. Instruments designed for devastation could contribute to prolonging prosperous life. It is certainly true that justice is helpless without supporting power. Given persons as they are and group conflict as it exists, deterrence may be the best policy possible. Any alternative policy would then be rejected because it could not achieve the ethical aims sought.

ARGUMENTS AGAINST DETERRENCE

There is also a strong case against a policy that relies primarily on military deterrence. Observations such as the following include both refutation of some of the previous claims as well as introduction of additional considerations.

1. Even at best, deterrence is a weak instrument for its purpose. On psychological and sociological grounds it can be argued that military threat has a limited motivational effect. The prospect of terror does not necessarily prevent terror. Deterrence relies on the threat of punishment. This has psychological limitations. As pointed out by one group of psychiatrists, "Punishment or the threat of it may inhibit an undesired form of behavior in individuals, but it tends to leave the underlying motivation unchanged and stimulates resentment toward the punitive agent. The result is that punished behavior reappears, perhaps even more strongly, after the threat of punishment is withdrawn."[1] Using armaments for bargaining power may have a short-run coercive effect at the same time that it stiffens an opponent's long-run resolve. When coerced on major matters considered of vital importance, nations will rebel at the first possible opportunity. A deterrence policy may postpone war at the same time that it makes hostilities eventually more certain as well as more destructive.

A more effective policy would incorporate larger measures of reward, adding an assortment of carrots to the stick. Such rewards both reinforce the desired behavior and create a favorable attitude toward the rewarding agent, thus further reducing incentive toward undesirable conduct.

Modern deterrence depends on a high level of fear and threat. Research suggests that too great a threat is likely to lead to "tunnel vision." Attention is concentrated on the threats to such an extent that other considerations are overlooked. Such simplistic thinking becomes irrational. In an attempt to escape the painful prospects of the present situation, it may produce a reactionary trend. This is an effort to turn the clock back to more secure times of the past. Such a reactionary policy is likely to make the present situation even worse. As the same group of psychiatrists put it, "Under the effects of fear, people are more prone to fall back on conventional and habitual responses that are no longer appropriate."[2] This is similar to the reaction of a theater crowd when fire breaks out. Most people tend to rush toward the main exit and to forget about other exits more easily available but less habitually used.

Or with some persons, intense fear may produce a kind of functional paralysis. Persons "freeze." Normal activity is slowed down or stopped, and rational thought becomes less possible. Coercion by serious military threat leads to deep anxiety. Acute anxiety tends to corrupt our responses, destroy our objectivity, and distort our observations. We act in ways contrary to the requirements of reality. During times of severe crisis, irrational acts may seem quite rational.

Deterrence policy depends on the assumption that people will react rationally and efficiently. Therefore when the results of war promise unacceptable damage, people will not start a war. Yet realistically speaking, even well-intentioned persons are finite. Those in control of a nation's policy can miscalculate or be misinformed about what will happen if their nation acts aggressively. Or because of their own deep desires they may easily engage in wishful thinking, attributing too great a probability to the outcome they most want. There are also neurotic persons who react defensively or compulsively in spite of the realities of any situation. They become less tolerant of ambiguity. They have a greater desire immediately to resolve the situation by some precipitate action. Winston Churchill in his classic "balance of terror" speech made what he himself called "a formidable admission." He said: "The deterrent does not cover the case of lunatics or dictators in the mood of Hitler when he found himself in his final dugout. That is a blank."[3]

2. Military deterrence as a way to peace can be seen as counterproductive. In direct contradiction to the aims of the policy, in several respects deterrence policies make wars more likely instead of less likely. The nature of the "solution" contributes to the problem. One reason for this is that military buildups cultivate instability by stimulating an arms race. When one country increases its strength, possible opponents respond by corresponding increases, which in turn must be matched by the first nation. This becomes a continuing action-reaction cycle or vicious circle—a vast international game of "Can you top this?" The security of country A becomes a source of insecurity for country B. What looks like deterrence to one side becomes a stimulus to military preparation for the other. No balance of international power remains stable. Nations do not lock their laboratories nor sedate the imaginations of their scientists. As Ernest Cuneo has put it, "It is as impossible to freeze a balance-of-power armament race as it is to freeze two race-horses pounding down the home stretch neck and neck for the Grand Prix."[4] Not only does such a weapons race not prevent war, but it makes war all the more destructive when it occurs.

At the same time such an acceleration in weaponry increases international tension, fear, suspicion, and hostility. In this atmosphere wars are more likely to occur. When a nation feels, even mistakenly, that it can do so with comparative immunity, it is even more likely to strike first—either in preventive war to keep another power from developing or in preemptive war if it is convinced that the other side is about to attack.

Whenever diplomacy becomes difficult, there is a temptation to use the military might that is waiting to be released. Or when things do not go well in even a comparatively minor war, there is the temptation to escalate toward nuclear war. Since machines do break down, systems for observation, communication, or missile launching all carry the possibility of accidental war. Human error or mental breakdown could produce a similar result. The more equipment we have, or the more nations that have nuclear weapons, the more likely such occurrences become. Seriously psychotic individuals are likely to be screened out of sensitive positions. But a more serious danger is presented by apparently normal people who can conceal their deep hostilities and suspicions, or the delight they take in destruction. Every person has a limited stress tolerance. Beyond that point, full rationality and control break down. Robert W. Gardiner therefore says, "The ultimate implication of this fact is that every single person, however 'normal,' who handles nuclear weapons, represents a potential accident."[5]

Furthermore, international tensions and fears in a real sense increase the strength of the very opposition we are trying to weaken. Instead of increasing the influence of doves in opposing nations, we strengthen the appeal of the hawks. Those demanding increases in armaments can always point to the missiles aimed at their fellow countrymen from beyond the borders. Instead of driving a wedge between the people of another country and their dictatorial or aggressive rulers, we help to solidify the regime and the people. We provide the external threat which dictators can use to consolidate their positions. To this extent we do the public relations work of the dictators for them.

At the same time that a desire for greater deterring power welds alliances together, there are important respects in which increasingly devastating weapons weaken the very alliances they are designed to protect. In contemporary times, allies incur greater risks. To carry out their obligations they may be called upon to participate in nuclear wars which will destroy their very existence. The "nuclear umbrella" may become more threatening than reassuring, especially for those countries which might feel the first impact of any attack. Because of the frightful effects of nuclear war, and because any war between superpowers fought with conventional weapons might escalate into nuclear dimensions, a smaller ally can no longer as confidently count on its protective superpower coming to its defense. The greater strength of our weapons has reduced the credibility of our alliances.

This increases the pressure on smaller nations to develop their own nuclear arsenals. The resulting spread of nuclear weapons carries possibilities for their use that can escape the force of deterrence policies. Proliferation of nuclear devices makes it possible to conceal more easily the source of a disabling attack. Deterrence depends on the ability to retaliate. But retaliation requires knowing where the attack came from. It is virtually impossible to determine the source of an attack when missiles are thrust from the sea by mobile submarines. More than that, even when nuclear submarines are not yet available to many nations, the scenario of the "suitcase attack" is realistic enough to give us shudders. Suppose a few nuclear devices were checked in baggage lockers or concealed in closets of downtown office buildings. When they exploded, the attacker would remain unidentified. If one major nuclear power so attacked assumed that its chief rival was the culprit, it might send its missiles flying in that direction. This might release the retaliation of the other major power. After the superpowers had decimated each other, the weaker nation that had planted the original bombs might conceivably move in to dominate what remained of the world.

Even without such bizarre though quite possible episodes, the basic international effects of deterrence policies in important ways make war more likely. To the popular belief that "one sword holds another in its sheath" must be added the Biblical insight that "all who take the sword will perish by the sword" (Matt. 26:52).

3. At the same time that it increases the dangers of war, primary reliance on a deterrence policy tends to undermine important positive bases for peace. The attempt to deter war does not get at the basic causes of conflict. It clamps the lid on the boiling pot without shutting off the gas. The necessary foundations for sustained peace include understanding, goodwill, agreement, and mutually beneficial interdependence. These are not cultivated by military preparation nor by the propaganda necessary to gain public support for heavy taxation for armaments.

Resolving conflicts in national interests requires the give-and-take of negotiation regarding economic, political, and military practices. But in an atmosphere of military standoff, nations are less likely to make significant concessions in negotiation, lest they be interpreted as a sign of national weakness. Traditional wisdom says that a nation should negotiate from a position of strength rather than from a position of weakness. When military considerations loom large, what is strength for one nation is weakness for others. In disarmament negotiations, for example, while one nation becomes more ready to parley, others become less ready. There is seldom, then, a right time to negotiate. A nation that feels it is behind in the arms race is afraid to negotiate, and a nation that is ahead feels that it does not need to.

Maintaining deterrence also obstructs the building of foundations for peace insofar as what is spent on armaments cannot be used for economic assistance in developing a decent life for the masses within the poor nations. Worldwide military expenditures are considerably greater than the total income of the poorer half of the world. The United States uses up each day for military purposes more than the entire annual budget of the UN World Food Program. Every twenty-nine hours our Department of Defense spends more than the UN Development Program has available in an entire year.[6] Our international priorities rob the poor of the world when God's resources were created for the most urgent needs of every person on earth. We deny our Christian stewardship for allocating the irreplaceable resources of the earth.

4. Nations deeply committed to a deterrence policy drastically reduce many of those total resources which presumably they are trying to defend. Armament is costly. In the modern world it requires a smothering, backbreaking budget. This inevitably reduces the measures that can be taken to deal with other social problems. Military expenditure contributes to inflation, the balance of payments problem, and high taxation. Solutions to all of these are also necessary for national strength. The cost of armament includes decaying cities, deteriorated countrysides, less breathable air, along with more poverty, ignorance, disease, crushed hopes, and lower morality. As President Dwight D. Eisenhower said to the American Society of Newspaper Editors in 1953, "Every gun that is made, every warship launched, every rocket fired signifies, in the final sense, a theft from those who hunger and are not fed, those who are cold and are not clothed."

We delay our development of more important social and spiritual values while we tie up our best brains in weapons production. Almost half of the world's scientists and engineers are employed directly or indirectly in military research and development. The developing nations desperately need higher standards of living for their populations, but their military expenditures are estimated to be doubling every six years.[7] William Epstein, former director of the disarmament division of the United Nations Secretariat, estimated that the world expenditure for armaments was "more than the total income of all the people of Africa, South Asia, and the Far East."[8] By destroying God's material gifts we reverse the process of creation. By diverting God's bounty from the poor and needy, we rebel against God's purposes. Richard J. Barnet has said, "The American people are devoting more resources to the war machine than is spent by all federal, state, and local governments on health and hospitals, education, old-age and retirement benefits, public assistance and relief, unemployment and social security, housing and community development, and the support of agriculture." Then he adds, "The result of this gigantic investment in security has been to make the American people among the most insecure on the planet."[9]

Diverting basic resources into lavish military expenditures is one of the surest ways for the United States to become a second-rate power. As we use up our natural resources, we hasten our dependence on foreign sources of supply and economically lose our international competitive advantage.[10] In addition to depletion of irreplaceable natural wealth, our current military priorities are responsible for much of our increase in pollution and general deterioration of the environment. Even if we were deterring nuclear destruction, we would also be hastening ecological destruction. Exhaustion of irreplaceable natural resources dooms succeeding generations to death as surely as if we exploded all our stockpiles of nuclear weapons.

Our military preoccupations are also becoming threats to democracy. Military responses to international emergencies may need to be made so suddenly as not to allow the delays of democratic decision. We once fought a revolutionary war against taxation without representation. If we continue our present infatuation with military deterrence, we may at some future time experience annihilation without representation. Furthermore, in order to project an image of maximum strength to other nations, we are tempted to demand a united front on foreign policy. It is easy, then, to regard agitation for alternative policies as distasteful or disloyal. At the same time we allocate more decision-making power to specialists in vast destruction concentrated in the military-industrial complex. Even though the civilian interest is constitutionally expected to control the military, we give large appropriations to the Pentagon to propagandize the American people.

There are other serious threats to freedom. An arms race demands considerable secrecy. A military arsenal requires protection against espionage and sabotage. As the bacteriological or nuclear components of modern weapons systems become more decisively destructive, the temptation becomes greater for guerrillas or saboteurs in sympathy with a hostile power. Providing security against such infiltration could become extremely difficult. The price of plutonium could possibly include a police state. As the arms race involves more centers for scientific and technological research, as the complexity of military hardware extends the network of industrial suppliers, as there are more points at which terrorists can seize small amounts of extremely destructive material and hold entire populations in hostage, the security measures thought necessary may become so thoroughgoing as to abrogate cherished civil liberties. Thereby we would lose the very freedoms our military power was intended to defend.

5. Another intolerable loss is serious enough to be listed separately. A disabling blow to our basic charac-

ter is the gradual moral deterioration of the nation that is amassing armaments. Reinhold Niebuhr once suggested that by the use of nuclear weapons the enemy might be physically destroyed, while the attacker was morally destroyed. In defense of private or national interests, or even of our own lives, how many millions are we justified in killing? How many centers of civilization may we destroy? Among our own citizens how many thousands may we shut out of scarce air-raid shelters or food-storage vaults? At what point do we ourselves become brutalized, dehumanized, and morally despicable? Even if we do not use the weapons we stockpile, we reap the consequences of knowing that at any moment we may become total destroyers.[11]

The process of developing more lethal weapons can be expected to erode our moral sensibilities. What we would have considered as an atrocity before, we come to accept as a necessary evil. By raising the number of deaths we are willing to accept for a given end, we depreciate the value of every single human life. We come to view dispassionately the most monstrous crimes against humanity. We calmly talk about "city swapping" with less thought about what concretely that would mean. By automating killing in electronic battlefields we detach ourselves from blame for pushing the buttons. The technological momentum of weaponry comes to outrun our moral indignation.[12] In many ways we have made evil routine, and harnessed our highest technological potency to wasteful and destructive processes.

6. As the trend continues toward more powerful weapons, their deterring power finally disappears. To understand this, consider the so-called "doomsday" machine, a theoretical weapon so potent that a single use of it would wipe all human life off the planet. Then imagine that each of two nations possessed a semi-doomsday

machine in that one single multiheaded missile could destroy life on half the earth. Suppose one nation used such a weapon on us and our allies, obliterating us except for one or two missile-bearing submarine or hardened launching sites. Should we then launch the weapon that would in retaliation destroy the other half of the world? No human value would be protected by the elimination of all human values. Ethically there would seem to be no justification for such an act of sheer revenge. Such retaliation would add to the physical obliteration of entire populations and to the moral annihilation of the attacker. If any nation were to make its last act before passing off the pages of history the extinction of human life, this would be, not a heroic episode, but such a reprehensible deed as to obscure whatever glory had characterized the previous history of that nation. The best possible action under the circumstances of this scenario would require allowing half the race to continue to live in the hope that through the centuries ahead the long climb of humanity toward freedom and justice might once again be attempted—this time with more success.

When such powerful weaponry is available, a potential aggressor might well conclude that there would be no likelihood of retaliation. Doomsday machines would lose their deterring power, for deterrence depends upon the expectation of retaliation. In our arsenals of annihilation, superpowers have already come close to doomsday capability. We have gone far beyond the "musket ball" dropped on Hiroshima. David Inglis has pointed out that a single modern bomb can deliver more explosive power than all the weapons used by all the nations for all purposes during all the wars of history.[13] Harrison Brown and James Real have written that if we represented the explosive power of a World War II blockbuster by a one-foot ruler, then "on this scale the bomb that demolished Hiroshima would be represented by the height of the Empire State building, and a twenty-megaton weapon by the height of the orbit of Sputnik I."[14]

While for the sake of immediate clarity we used above the illustration of the doomsday machine, we already face the same problem with presently available weapons. After an attack has been received, retaliation may serve no purpose other than a further devastation of values. If the purpose of our nuclear weapons had been to deter attack, they would then have no further purpose to serve. They would already have failed to deter. If the purpose of our nuclear weapons was also to protect other social values for our citizens, and if those values were already substantially destroyed by the enemy's first strike, then also retaliation would make little sense. It would lose its moral justification.

We may already have reached the time, certainly we are nearing it, when, having achieved the greatest physical power ever known to humanity, we will also have moved into our period of maximum vulnerability and weakness. The weapons in which we trusted can then be used neither for attack nor for deterrence. As Harlan Cleveland said of nuclear weapons, "In day to day politics, they are not even very useful for brandishing."[15] As the strength of military deterrents approaches infinity, our security will approach zero. As the technology of warfare moves toward the ultimate weapon, at some point it loses the capacity to defend.

This should come as no surprise to any serious student of ethics. We should know that there are points of diminishing returns in values, beyond which indulgence becomes evil instead of good. Food is necessary for health, but in excess destroys health. Higher standards of living may liberate human potentialities, until the point is reached at which they produce lethargy for the rich who enjoy them and starvation for the poor at whose expense they are enjoyed. That which is medicine in measured doses becomes poison in larger consumption. Parents may use some punishment to motivate socially desirable behavior. Minor theft may be followed by deprivation of allowance or even by spanking. But if these attempts at coercion are ineffective and the stealing becomes worse, an escalation of sanctions becomes utterly self-defeating. To cut off the child's right arm would arouse such resentment and rebellion as to destroy all possibility of accepting the desired social standard.

If we have not already reached the point of counter-productivity in weaponry, we are certainly close to it. Giving deterrence policies all possible benefit of the doubt, they have always been inefficient instruments for their purpose. We should have been able to do better. Now we are rapidly approaching the point at which they can no longer be defended at all. To avoid unimaginable calamity we *must* do better. What was always dubious in the light of ethical norms of justice and love is now becoming indefensible. Obedience to God and concern for humankind require an alternative foreign policy. What is now going on between the nations is reciprocal insanity. A synonym for modern deterrence is mutually assured destruction. Appropriately the acronym for "mutually assured destruction" is MAD. The most unrealistic people are those who believe we can continue as we are. Sociological sophistication, planetary realism, and theological responsibility support the 1968 statement of the General Board of the National Council of Churches concerning our foreign policy: "The necessary changes require first that we stop thinking in obsolete terms."

As prominent an exponent of political realism as Hans Morgenthau has concluded that nuclear weapons "are not susceptible to rational use as instruments of national policy. . . . The immensity of the military force which the nuclear age has generated goes hand in hand with the devaluation of its practical use. The more endowed a nation is with military force, the less it is able to use it."[16] Ramsey Clark agrees that "no increment in the offensive or defensive nuclear systems of a nation large or small can offer protection. . . . The balancing act is over, for the weight of weaponry created by technology has crushed the scales."[17] Nuclear weapons become not only suicidal but also genocidal. Jerome Wiesner and Herbert York, two scientists who served as presidential advisers to both Eisenhower and Kennedy, concluded: "Both sides in the arms race are thus confronted by the dilemma of heavily increasing military power and steadily decreasing national security. . . . The clearly predictable course of the arms race is a steady open spiral downward into oblivion."[18]

IMPLICATIONS FOR NATIONAL POLICY

This is not to say that no degree of armament is now defensible. In our world of sharp divisions, nationalistic loyalties, capabilities for destruction or blackmail, and populations untrained in nonviolent resistance methods, some sort of armament level is clearly needed. It still may be required for some years. However, a responsible level of military strength does not need to retain our present overkill capacity. Responsible authorities insist that we have enough armament to obliterate our major opponents several times over. Adding still more contributes nothing to our security. On the contrary, it adds to our peril by draining resources from other needs, diverting us from basic causes of international conflict and contributing to the continued instability of the arms race. Are we interested in the welfare of the poor, the reduction of crime, better schools, more economic aid for the developing world? All these become possible by significant reductions in our vast military expenditures. Our cutting back not only on bureaucratic wastes but also on what is genuinely unnecessary overkill would leave us no worse off in national defense and could leave us considerably better off in other aspects of national strength. Through long established habit the American people are deeply impressed by the risk of disarmament. We need to see more clearly the risks of unnecessary armament, not only to ourselves but to our total physical environment and to the entire human race. A defensible amount of disarmament now becomes a contribution to our security.

A limited arms reduction by the United States, if carefully and wisely done, could stimulate a similar response by the Soviet Union. Unless Russian leaders did likewise, they would be unnecessarily draining their own natural resources, increasing the burden of privation on the Soviet people, and losing influence among other nations which desired a lower level of armament.

A beginning step on our part might be set within the framework of the graduated reciprocal initiatives policy proposed by Charles Osgood and others.[19] The suggestion is that the United States take limited but significant steps to reduce armament or international tensions, announcing that further unilateral steps will be taken if the Soviet Union reciprocates. Each initiative would be small enough not seriously to endanger our security. For this reason the strong argument against immediate complete unilateral disarmament outlined above does not apply to the unilateral initiatives proposal. Successive steps on both sides could then become cumulative and of increased significance. Each successful cycle would contribute to an international climate which would make the next cycle easier.

Neither the United States nor the Soviet Union has seriously pursued such a policy, though there have been isolated instances suggesting what might be done. United Nations disarmament specialist William Epstein reports that in 1963–1964 both the United States and the Soviet Union made armament budget reductions "not by agreement, but by what Khrushchev called 'the policy of mutual example.' "[20] Amitai Etzioni further reports unilateral initiatives during that period which were reciprocated and which contributed to more fruitful negotiation.[21] The development of such a peace offensive might become the persuasive equivalent of army exercises and naval maneuvers. As Osgood pointed out, "We need to play peace games just as seriously as we play war games."[22] By such means, along with other policy changes about to be mentioned, the vicious circle of the arms race may still be reversed into a benign cumulative spiral of increasing disarmament. The arms race might become a peace race. Along with other major international changes, this could move toward the more distant day when nations would find better sources of security, including monitored and controlled universal and complete disarmament with only small domestic and international police forces. There are more promising political, economic, and international options which may replace those features of our foreign policy that have become obsolete in the light of contemporary realities. The rest of this book will be devoted largely to directions for such innovation.

7

Political Structures
of Interdependence

CHRISTIANS UNDERSTAND something about the unity of humanity under God. Their faith gives them a sense of responsibility for their neighbors in other countries and an appreciation of the dignity of all human beings on all sides of the political lines that divide them. Christians should therefore be concerned about the development of institutions that give expression to the human solidarity implied in those convictions. Patriotism has an important place among human virtues, but its claims are limited and it should be seen as subordinate to higher and wider loyalties. Political nationalism has a role to play. This is especially so when a national community is seeking to be free from domination by outside powers, when it strives to establish and protect its own identity and its own distinctive character, and when it seeks to transmit from generation to generation the particular treasures of its own culture and tradition. But nationalism carries with it the temptation to make one's own national community an absolute, an idol that distorts one's view of people on the other side of the boundary and poisons the relations between nations. Nations, and not least our own, are tempted by self-righteousness in relation to most of the world. Among the great powers there is often an articulate minority that is governed by a chauvinistic type of nationalism that glories in the nation's military power. We are convinced that in the United States this is a small though vociferous minority.

THE LIMITS OF THE BALANCE OF POWER

We have referred from time to time to the extent to which anarchy exists among nations today. They live under no enforceable international law. They are ultimately insecure in their relations with one another. The only source of security that has been much trusted by the stronger powers has been the so-called balance of power. When Europe in terms of power was at the center of the world, this balance of power was preserved for many generations by England. When nations on the Continent were threatened by defeat in war, England supported them, thus preventing one nation or alliance from becoming dominant on the Continent. The United States in the two world wars took part in this balancing process. But after the second war the old Europe-centered pattern was broken. Not only did the United States and the Soviet Union seek to balance each other as centers of alliances, but the nations of Asia, Africa, and Latin America introduced new forms of power, creating forms of global instability that in modern times had never existed before. The struggle to preserve some kind of balance between the United States and the Soviet Union goes on. But this has led to complicated maneuvers that involve new American relations with both China and the Soviet Union and a continuous activity to contain conflicts that might spread to the major powers. Each side in the cold war has tried to counteract the efforts of the other to gain support from nations that are new actors on the world scene.

The balance of power is never stable, because nations are always trying to upset it in their favor. Today the number of international actors has grown and the varieties of power have greatly increased. There is the intangible power of anticolonial resentment, and the power of revolutionary movements within nations that have influence beyond their borders, and the economic power such as that of the OPEC (Organization of Petroleum Exporting Countries) nations. These have created a situation of instability and unpredictability which make the balance of power as a means of preserving the security of nations unreliable. This does not mean that it is unimportant to have a wider distribution of power than is now present in the world. Together with what we call structures of interdependence, such a distribution would be favorable to peace and to the prevention of world domination by one nation or one group of nations.[1]

NECESSITY OF INTERNATIONAL INSTITUTIONS OF WORLD ORDER

This briefly describes the complexities we face as we attempt to move away from anarchy, away from idolatrous nationalism, away from the absoluteness of national sovereignty, away from the constant threat of war. There are no policies which are either Christian in an absolute sense or exclusively Christian. But Christians, along with all persons of goodwill, have the responsibility to find policies that move toward structures of worldwide community. Some policies are more compatible with Christian ethics than others; some are antithetical to Christian ethics. We have mentioned "all persons of goodwill," but many more can contribute than those who are conscious of the kind of altruistic commitment which those words suggest. The survival of nations is at stake, perhaps the very survival of the human race. One ground for hope is the convergence of the claims of loyalty to the larger good, of love for all neighbors, and the kind of prudence for which the conditions for survival prepare all who are not blinded by hatred and inherited irrational feuds or by ideology.

We have used the word "interdependence," and we hope that its realities will dawn on people on all sides. Interdependence includes areas that go far beyond the political relations between states. All nations depend upon the same global environment, upon the same oceans and the same biosphere, upon material resources that are more limited now than any previous generation could imagine. The future of nations will also depend upon control of the world's population. No nation has the power to escape from a common human fate.

There is a strong tendency in Christian theology, which often takes one-sided forms, to give religious support to government especially insofar as it is responsible for order. Romans 13:1–7 and I Peter 2:13–15 are often quoted to support the Christian's duty to obey the political authorities. Almost always in modern times, because of the historical circumstances, these verses have been used to give sanction to national governments as providential agents. As a rule churches within nations have used these religious principles in behalf of their own national governments in international affairs in both peace and war without keeping them under rigorous criticism when they engaged in narrowly nationalistic or even chauvinist actions. Today Christians and churches are better prepared to offer such criticism. They see that the sovereign nation-state which preserves order within a nation too often becomes an agent of disorder in the international sphere. Because of this the religious sanctions given under Biblical guidance should be shared with the emerging institutions of world order. These institutions do not yet have ways of establishing their authority over nation-states, but they have moral claims and nascent legal claims which Christians and churches should be the first to recognize.

At the end of the Second World War the American

churches that were associated with the Federal Council of Churches (one of several predecessors of the National Council of Churches) made an enormous effort, on both a denominational and an ecumenical basis, to move the nation to support the United Nations. This effort began during the war in order to prevent the United States from relapsing into isolationism at the war's end, as had happened in the case of our refusal to join the League of Nations at the end of the First World War. As far as we know, there had never before been such a concerted attempt on the part of churches in this country to influence foreign policy. They were successful, though credit for American support of the United Nations must be shared by many other movements and institutions.

Support for the United Nations by American public opinion and specifically by the churches has continued to the present time. Failure of the United Nations to accomplish all that had been hoped and criticisms of particular actions by it have reduced the percentage of supporters and also the intensity of their loyalty. We have referred to Professor Seyom Brown's statement that "the 1972 polls registered 63 percent agreeing with the proposition that 'the United States should cooperate fully with the United Nations' (down only 9 percentage points since 1964)." This is still good evidence of what the American people would like to believe about the United Nations even though the percentage of full support has dropped since 1972 to 49 percent as opposed to 41 percent who withhold that support. This is still a majority of those who have opinions. This sudden drop in support is caused in considerable measure by actions of the United Nations in regard to Israel, especially the resolution identifying Zionism with racism in 1976.[2]

Pope John XXIII in his encyclical *Pacem in Terris* (1963) went all out in his support for international institutions. He said the following: "Today the universal common good poses problems of world-wide dimensions which cannot be adequately tackled or solved except by efforts of public authorities endowed with a breadth of powers, structure and means of the same proportions: that is, of public authorities which are in a position to act in an effective manner on a world-wide basis. The moral order itself, therefore, demands that such a form of public authority be established" (par. 137). Later the pope added the following: "It is our earnest prayer that the United Nations—in its structure and means—may become ever more equal to the magnitude and nobility of its tasks" (par. 145).

Before the Second World War had ended there was in this country much discussion of the kind of world that would come after it. Predictions that were made had little to do with subsequent developments because people did not foresee the decades of cold war. Also the extent to which the world would be changed by the emergence of newly independent nations in Asia and Africa was not imagined. In many circles there was hope that after the war it would be possible to establish a world government with enough power over sovereign states to control relations between them so as to prevent war. Many schemes were proposed and some went so far as to envisage a world government that would have considerable authority over citizens within nations. The main interest, however, was war prevention.

WORLD GOVERNMENT AND MORE LIMITED APPROACHES

There were two conceptions of the hoped-for world government. One was that it should consist only of democratic nations mostly in the Atlantic area. This was because common bonds existed among them, mutual trust was possible, and similar political practices could be projected onto a wider stage. The other concept was of a universal world government in spite of the obvious difficulties. The more limited scheme was thought to be in danger of hardening an alliance of like-minded nations against those which would become an opposing camp. Such a situation, it seemed, might even lead to the war that a world government would be designed to prevent.

The scheme of universal world government that was limited to the purpose of war prevention which came to arouse most interest was written by Grenville Clark and Louis B. Sohn under the title *World Peace Through World Law,* in 1958.[3] This called for a system of enforceable world law involving an executive council, a court of law, and a world assembly in which votes would depend on the size of the populations of the nations. A sidelight on the difficulty of devising such an assembly based upon the representation of populations was that all nations with populations of more than 140 million were to have the same number of votes. If this scheme had been published in Peking or New Delhi rather than in Cambridge, Massachusetts, the figures would have been vastly different! This scheme presupposed universal disarmament, for only so could the police power of the world government be stronger than the military power of the stronger nations. This scheme so impressed Herman Kahn that he suggested that after the first exchange of bombs in a possible war between the United States and the Soviet Union "the President of the United States might send a copy of this book to Premier Khrushchev saying: 'there is no point in your reading this book; you will not like it any more than I did. I merely suggest that you sign it, right after my signature. This is the only plan that has been roughly thought through; let us therefore accept it. We surely do not wish to set up a commission to study other methods of organizing the world, because within weeks both of us will be trying to exploit our common danger for unilateral advantages. If we are to have a settlement, we must have it now, before the dead are buried.' "[4] That is a tribute to the extent to which the scheme does give substance to a widely hoped for form of world organization.

After the Second World War the effort to create a new structure for the world took the form of the United Nations. This was far removed from schemes of world government. It was not a supergovernment with power over member nations. Under some conditions it was envisaged that either the Security Council or the General Assembly would be able to bring considerable pressure on states. It was also hoped that this pressure might in the case of dangerous conflicts involve the use of economic or even limited military power. In fact, its power has been chiefly moral though it has created situations in which the settlement of disputes or the shortening of wars was facilitated. The United Nations was not limited to democracies, nor was it universal. It began with the wartime alliance that included the Soviet Union and its allies. Only gradually has it been extended to include nations that had been enemies in the war, and only later has it come to include nations such as the People's Republic of China, which one side in the cold war for many years voted to exclude. The United Nations is not limited to war prevention. Its Economic and Social Council and its specialized agencies enter into many fields of international cooperation. We shall return to the significance of the United Nations later.

Here we want to point out that the interest in full-blown world government has declined. The life of the world has become not only complex, but so complex that it is difficult to think of managing it by any political superstructure. Not only have the most ambitious schemes for world government that might supplant the United Nations lost support, but also the very idea of a system of collective security as was envisaged by the League of Nations, has in our time seemed to lose feasibility. The failure of the League and of experiments between the wars to create a tight system of collective security belong to the background of the present tendency to think in more modest terms of world organization.

There was an article that must be something of a landmark among supporters of the more ambitious schemes of worldwide federalism. Donald Keyes had given most of his career to this cause and at the time of the publication of the article was the "non-governmental" representative of the World Association of World Federalists at the United Nations. He speaks of a "functional" approach to world federalism. He says that "there are no more illusions about the ease of convincing governments to relinquish national sovereignty. States will agree to limitations in unilateral decision-making only to the extent that it is painfully necessary —and maybe not even then." He says: "Federalists are now recognizing that the world community is in fact beginning to establish a series of global departments to deal with specific global tasks. Instead of the vertical or hierarchical structure which has been the presupposition and vision of early Federalists—we see a horizontal proliferation of organs to perform specialized functions. Federalists no longer have the luxury of seeking a neat and orderly solution to world governance."[5] Statements like this almost take one's breath away if one has been involved in the early postwar discussion of world federalism as over against the more limited structures and procedures of the United Nations.

Writing out of a background of deep commitment to the United Nations, Professor Richard Gardiner has helpfully summarized the changed expectations about forms of worldwide institutions: "The hope for the foreseeable future lies, not in building up a few ambitious central institutions of universal membership and general jurisdiction as was envisaged at the end of the last war, but rather in a much more decentralized, disorderly and pragmatic process of inventing or adapting institutions of limited jurisdiction and selected membership to deal with specific problems on a case by case basis, as the necessity of cooperation is perceived by the relevant nations."[6]

This approach should be regarded as a way in which the sovereignty of nations may be limited through arriving at particular agreements in relation to urgent problems. Those engaged in this process need to be guided by the vision of a more ordered world even though they avoid total schemes for world government. They also should be guided by warnings against the danger of a centralized world government. With a monopoly of decisive nuclear power it could become tyrannical and invite revolutionary efforts to control the center which might involve civil wars within the structured worldwide community.

Reinhold Niebuhr on World Government

While the postwar discussion of forms of world government was at its height Reinhold Niebuhr published an article in 1949 entitled "The Illusion of World Government."[7] This article had immense influence both in the churches and outside. Its conclusions corresponded with the thinking within the churches expressed in a series of conferences on World Order sponsored by the Federal Council of Churches and later by the National Council of Churches. The American churches that were concerned about organizing the world for peace generally supported the approach embodied in the United Nations rather than schemes of world government.

In his article Niebuhr summarized the obstacles to establishing a world government with decisive power over nation-states in the following words: "The fallacy of world government can be stated in two simple propositions. The first is that governments are not created by fiat (though sometimes they can be imposed by tyranny). The second is that governments have only limited efficacy in integrating a community."

Niebuhr also discussed what he called "the social tissues of the world community." He recognized that there are three such tissues: the increasing economic interdependence, the common fear of mutual annihilation, and the "inchoate sense of obligation to the inchoate community of mankind." When he wrote he was especially concerned about the complete lack of mutual trust between Communist countries and those in "the free world." Perhaps today we may regard as more serious in the long run the lack of mutual trust between have and have-not nations. Niebuhr showed how difficult it is to achieve a sense of community that is sufficiently binding to give moral and political support to world government. Yet in 1952 he was able to say, not because conditions were better in that year but as an expression of a hopefulness, that he never lost: "Undoubtedly the constitutional instruments of world order must be perfected in time. But the more perfect instruments must grow out of the more perfect mutualities of daily living together." He was a strong supporter of the United Nations. He saw it as the means by which this "daily living together" may be made possible. He saw the United Nations as a precarious bridge between the two sides in the cold war. He also saw in the United Nations a forum in which American power might be kept under criticism from friends as well as from adversaries. He welcomed the fact that "we have become part and parcel of a world community which has its own inchoate organs for integrating a common mind and expressing a common will. Fortunately our decision will be part of a wider decision of an international community."[8] These quotations suggest that in 1952, Niebuhr did have a sense of the open-endedness of the structures of the United Nations.

Since Niebuhr wrote, sources of conflict between nations, especially between the rich and poor nations, have become more profound. There are, however, new tissues of community developing, especially as nations are forced to deal with recently understood threats to the common environment, and as they struggle together to find some agreements concerning access to resources as in the case of those in the seabed. It would be as much an error to allow preconceived limits to the formation of tissues of community to inhibit action, as it would be to be guided by illusory expectations.

Niebuhr's first proposition that "governments are not created by fiat" is the more tangible and brings out more clearly the obstacles to world government with centralized power over the nations. We shall elaborate this in the following way. A constitution-making fiat cannot change the location of the main centers of power in the world. Consider these sources of power: the size of the population, natural resources and the technological and economic use of them, effective political institutions, the morale of a people, and the state of military technology and organization. These, or at least several of them, must go together. Population without resources, for example, can be a source of weakness rather than of power. The nations that have a good combination of these sources of power will still have them whatever structure of world government may be established. For that structure to have enough central military power to limit the military activity of states that are at present militarily powerful would call for disarmament of those states. This cannot be compelled.

The founders of the League of Nations in articles 10 and 16 of the Covenant tried to set up a pooling of power. In case of aggression, the League would apply forceful economic and military sanctions against any state, no matter how powerful, that was guilty of aggression. But when it came to the crunch, as in the aggression of Mussolini's Italy against Ethiopia, states failed to apply the legally required sanctions. The League was dissolved as the Second World War approached. After that war, the United Nations in allowing the veto by permanent members of the Security Council reflected the realities of power in the world. Without that provision for the veto neither the United States nor the Soviet Union would have joined the United Nations. Also, without that provision the implementation of any coercive action attempted by the Security Council might well have caused the third world war between the two strongest powers.

THE UNITED NATIONS

We shall now deal with the frustrations, the achievements, and the important potentialities of the United Nations. Four things should be said at the outset.

1. If the United Nations did not exist, something very like it would need to be established now. This is true for many reasons. As a start we mention the need to have a center for constant communication between representatives of the nations, the need to have a sounding board for ideas and information concerning international issues, and the need for the initiation and coordination of innumerable multilateral activities which take place now under the UN umbrella. Without the United Nations the nations would be at a great disadvantage.

2. We should be aware of the default by the United States at important points in relation to the United Nations. Charles W. Yost, who was from 1961 to 1966 this country's Deputy Representative to the United Nations and from 1969 to 1971 its Permanent Representative, has written a book *The Conduct and Misconduct of Foreign Affairs.*[9] His verdict regarding U.S. participation is devastating. He writes: "The basic difficulty was that neither President Johnson nor President Nixon had any real respect for the United Nations. Both preferred to conduct their foreign affairs in the most unilateral and uninhibited manner they could get away with, and to resort to the U.N. only when they were reasonably certain it would support their position, or when they wished, as in the cases of Vietnam and Pakistan, to shift the blame for what had gone wrong. Even worse, by demanding that the United Nations do what it was not strong enough to do, or what a large majority of its members were opposed to its doing, and then denouncing its failure to act, these Presidents seriously undermined among Congress and the public the steadfast U.S. support of the United Nations which is indispensable to its health and growth." Yost is not only as well informed a witness as we could have, but in this and other writings he has shown himself to be a wise and sensitive commentator on international affairs.

3. The United States, which once controlled a majority in the United Nations, should now be prepared to accept defeat on issues from time to time. When President Johnson appointed Ambassador Arthur Goldberg to represent this country in the United Nations there seemed a possibility that the United Nations might help us to get out of Vietnam. The Security Council could not act but would it not have been good policy to have allowed the Assembly to act? Our government was obviously afraid of defeat. If the Assembly had directed the

United States to withdraw from Vietnam, this might have provided a face-saving alternative for a proud nation and a proud President. At that time the Assembly had more moral authority in this country than it had later because of such actions as the resolution about Zionism.

4. We need to examine any act that has brought the United Nations into some disrepute, such as the resolution about Zionism. Was what was done the fault of the United Nations as such or merely a reflection of the situation in the world which would be a problem even if there were no United Nations? There is, for example, the problem of the near isolation of Israel which the United Nations dramatizes but did not create.

What we have said about the limited power of the United Nations in contrast to the power of an imagined world government would lead one to expect that its chief influence on events would be indirect, educational, and moral. Yet we want to point out that the United Nations, especially when the United States and the Soviet Union were either indifferent to issues or in agreement, has many achievements involving direct control of events to its credit.

Professor Morgenthau summarizes its achievements of truces or peace settlements in the following passage: "There is no unmistakable evidence to show that the United Nations has prevented any war. There is, however, unmistakable evidence to show that it has materially contributed to the shortening of four wars: in Indonesia in 1949, in Palestine in 1949, in Egypt in 1956, and in Kashmir in 1965."[10]

The United Nations supervised the process by which the state of Israel came into existence through the partition of Palestine. It has provided a peacekeeping force that has been a buffer between adversaries several times in the Middle East, including the forces now present in Cyprus, between Israel and Egypt, and between Israel and Syria. Actions by the United Nations in the Middle East have done most to erode its support in the eyes of Americans. Yet today its presence there is helping to keep the peace. Amid all the turmoil and debate about the relations between Israel and her Arab neighbors there is widespread agreement that any enduring peace in the area will have to be based on the UN Security Council Resolution 242 that was passed on November 22, 1967. The United Nations sent observers to Lebanon in connection with a conflict there in 1958 and, according to Professor Leland M. Goodrich, this "played a significant role in bringing about the withdrawal of United States forces and the establishment of stability in the area."[11] (Unfortunately today there is no more tormented country than Lebanon.) The United Nations provided a peacekeeping force that facilitated the transfer of West Irian to Indonesia in 1962 after having had much to do with the establishment of Indonesia as an independent state in 1949.

The most ambitious and expensive operation was in the Congo where the United Nations kept a peacekeeping force in 1960 to bring order in that country after the departure of the Belgians. This involved intervention in a civil war in which the Soviet Union and the United States took sides. This operation became as controversial as it was extensive. Dr. Ernest Lefever in his study for The Brookings Institution says that on balance it was a contribution to the peace and security of Central Africa. He makes one observation that has great importance for the future of multilateral peacekeeping. He emphasizes the surprising degree of unity within the UN force which was gathered from many nations.[12] Years after the Congo operation Charles Yost, the fairness of whose judgment on matters connected with the

United Nations has impressed us, wrote that this was "one of the most effective peace-keeping operations."[13]

The action of the United Nations in Korea was made possible by the temporary absence of the Soviet Union from meetings of the Security Council. The defense of South Korea against North Korea was carried on by the United States with the sanction of the United Nations. Until the UN forces crossed the 38th parallel this action was widely hailed as an example of multilateral defense of a nation against aggression. The whole operation became problematic and lost much of its multilateral legitimacy as a police action when the war was extended into North Korea to the border of China. It does not seem to be a precedent for future action by the United Nations.

The United Nations could enter a new stage of existence if, as a result of the tapering off of the cold war, the United States and the Soviet Union as members of the Security Council were to have more common ground. The organization is there to be used. One example of such use might be to transfer to the United Nations the responsibility to police disarmament agreements which it is hoped may come out of negotiations between the two major nuclear powers.

If the conflict between East and West could be resolved, we might expect the United Nations to become the setting for many conflicts between North and South. There are many grievances between the rich industrial nations and the poor nations that regard themselves as victims of political colonialism in the past, and of economic colonialism in the present. The Assembly of the United Nations now has a majority of states that represent this anticolonial resentment. They do not present a united front and conflicts over their issues may be more complex than those between East and West. The size of the Assembly, the one nation-one vote rule, and the presence of many so-called ministates that have the same vote as the populous and powerful states—these factors are responsible for much of the current American frustration concerning the United Nations. Since most of those votes are cast against our government's position, our frustration is even greater. It is difficult to persuade delegations to use their votes to change the system and thus deprive those small nations of their present voting power. We have no idea what changes may prove possible. In the meantime the Assembly does provide a forum in which the needs and aspirations and resentments of the whole of humanity are expressed.

In the immediate future we believe that we may see the United Nations in its proper context if we grasp the full extent of its more indirect contribution to the politics of world community, to the politics of peace. Several of the most significant contributions of the United Nations are of this sort.

1. The Charter and such official statements of values as the Declaration of Human Rights hold up before humanity moral standards by which the conduct of nations will continue to be judged no matter how far they depart from them. They can be appealed to as the basis for investigating the facts about international conduct. It is no mere platitude to announce that nations should be judged by the principle "that all Members shall refrain in their international relations from the threat or use of force against the territorial integrity or political independence of any state or in any other manner inconsistent with the Purposes of the United Nations" (Charter, article 2). Throughout history it has been the habit of nations to make war on one another. Rationalizations for making the war were legion, and the glorification of war by the citizens of each nation was easy to accept. Partly because of the nature of modern war, and also because aspirations for a humane world of peace-

ful relations between peoples are more widely felt than ever before, any nation that makes war today is on the moral defensive in the world at large and sometimes before its own people.

The Charter also recognizes that conditions of injustice are an obstacle to peace. It is tragic that ideological conflicts concerning roads to justice and peace have so deeply separated people who share many of the same values as goals. The Declaration of Human Rights announces the claims of both individual and social rights upon all people. Individual rights include the right to freedom of thought, conscience, and religion, and the right to a fair trial. Social and economic rights include the right to work under just and favorable conditions, and the right to social security. It is surprising that the Assembly committed itself to both kinds of rights when so many nations represented still deny them to their own people. But these standards have real if precarious power over minds and consciences. Again, they form the basis for ferreting out the truth about the condition of peoples who are denied these rights.

Professor Goodrich, after thirty years of reflection on the United Nations and its effectiveness, says in the most recent of his several books on the subject that in spite of the generality of the statement of values in the Charter: "There is reason to believe that members of the United Nations have been substantially influenced in their policies and actions by the purposes and principles set forth in the Charter and by the interpretations given them by the organs of the United Nations."[14] That is an important claim. It deserves study by those who because of what may be overreaction to particular events have lost faith in the United Nations.

2. The United Nations provides opportunities for continuous contact between representatives of member nations. This makes informal diplomacy possible in crises

and before crises begin. It also makes possible friendly relations and even mutual trust between persons across boundaries of nation and even of ideology. The United Nations is coming near to being universal, and bridges can be built and maintained in many directions. Public diplomacy in speeches in the Security Council and the Assembly has its values, but it also tends to encourage both propaganda and hardened positions. The more informal diplomacy of everyday contact is a needed corrective for the drawbacks of public diplomacy. It can make new initiatives possible toward the resolution of conflict.

3. The public meetings provide forums for the expression of opinion. In spite of all the propaganda and the instances of polarization it is still possible to give voice to widely held public convictions. There is much cynicism about this at present, but these meetings do make possible the participation of persons who are neutral, more detached than those involved in conflict. For one thing, representatives of small and middle-sized states, who have their own gifts of wisdom and their own independent insight, can make important contributions to the discussions. The fact that the secretaries-general of the United Nations have all been citizens of small states (Norway, Sweden, Burma, and Austria) and have been able to retain a measure of independence from the rival blocs is of extreme importance. If the only persons who could receive a hearing in the world were statesmen representing the vested interests of great powers, the resources of wisdom or skill or moral influence for solving problems would be greatly reduced.

4. The processes of the United Nations can at times help proud nations to save face when they can yield to a collective voice of an organ of the United Nations rather than to adversaries. Hans Morgenthau has emphasized this point in the following words: "Thus na-

tions in conflict with each other can afford to do vis-à-vis the United Nations what they think that they cannot afford to do in their relations with each other—make concessions in the formulation, if not in the substance, of their policies without losing face. This is particularly so if the face-saving formula is proposed by a 'neutral' nation or group of nations."[15] The continuous informal diplomacy that we have mentioned will often make neutrals more effective. Personal relations help national leaders to understand each other well enough to know how others can be helped to make concessions in the light of public opinion at home.

5. The establishment of the Economic and Social Council as one of the chief organs of the United Nations and the proliferation of specialized agencies dealing with economic and social problems show how broad the United Nations is. It is more than an agency concerned about the political problems of security and peace. Social and economic problems have great political importance. They require the initiation of many activities in their own context. Some of the specialized agencies coordinate what states are already doing in such things as the control of aviation and postal services. At the same time, they make it possible for states to do what otherwise they could not do. Some of the specialized agencies call for new initiatives in raising the standards of employment (ILO), in the improvement of agriculture (FAO), in controlling the use of atomic energy (IAEA), in raising standards of health (WHO). UNESCO has been one of the best known of the agencies, and it has greatly stimulated intellectual exchange between nations. UNICEF has carried on extensive relief activities in many areas. Also it has done much to educate people in the more prosperous countries concerning the needs of children in poor countries.

In recent years there has been an enormous increase

of worldwide consultations on both old and new issues related to social justice, to the development of resources and to the control of technology. The United Nations, as we write, may be most important as the inspirer of concern and the organizer of worldwide public opinion on these issues. World conferences devoted to them—some of which have given rise to continuing agencies—have had a great deal of publicity. The following list of a few of them gives some idea of the scope of this side of the work of the United Nations: the Conference on the Human Environment in Stockholm (1972), the World Population Conference in Bucharest (1974), the World Food Conference in Rome (1974), the International Women's Year Conference in Mexico City (1975), and the Conference on Human Settlements in Vancouver (1976). Related to the control of resources is the series of sessions of negotiating conferences on the law of the sea and the control of the seabed by the nations with conflicting claims.

A creative corollary of these UN events is the unofficial conferences and activities of nongovernmental organizations (NGO's) which parallel the official meetings. Representing more directly human and social interests, they are often more pioneering and stimulating than the official conferences and add to their effectiveness and to follow-up activities.

There are many more ramifications of the activities of the United Nations, but these examples illustrate our main point. These conferences may not result in new policies by nations. Sometimes they may have seemed to end in stalemates. But they have stirred the minds of millions of people all over the world. In some cases as in the Rome Conference on Food, governments—especially the United States—were put on the defensive. It is impossible to estimate the results of all of this discussion but it needed to be stimulated. Ideas need to reverberate around the world before there can be more definite preparations for action. As Professor Nye says of these conferences, they were "largely exercises in agenda setting."[16] He also suggests that one of the effects of conferences of this kind is to strengthen agencies in a government which are committed to particular objectives, such as environmental protection, in their debates with other departments of the same government. He opens up a new horizon when he says: "The political importance of international organization, particularly on interdependence issues, is less in their power *above* states than in their role in coordinating bits and pieces of power *across* states."[17]

The issues of national security, of war and peace, are as fateful as ever but these are much affected in the long run by problems of justice, of the availability of resources, and the like. Some conflicts on the political front may be eased by cooperation on other fronts. Some struggles between nations over economic issues may have more constructive results if they are continually discussed on this agenda of the United Nations.

If new issues come to convince even the reluctant that survival requires global controls to protect such things as the biosphere or to save scarce resources, the United Nations is in place to be strengthened and to be used.

8

Rethinking America's Political Role in the World

WE HAVE REFERRED in Chapter 3 to the erosion of the postwar consensus that dominated American foreign policy for more than twenty-five years. The United States had emerged from the Second World War as by far the most powerful nation in the world. It had been militarily successful in Europe and in relation to Japan. The Soviet Union, also a victor in war, had been weakened by its enormous losses. Western Europe was grateful for American help both in war and in reconstruction. The fact that our country did not pursue a vindictive policy in either Europe or Asia added to its moral influence. If anyone today doubts that we were not vindictive when we had the power, the present prosperity of Japan and West Germany is sufficient evidence for this claim. This foreign policy consensus soon was controlled by our preoccupation with the cold war, by an obsessive anti-Communism.

This anti-Communism had at least two elements, and the question as to which was primary in importance is much debated. One was revulsion against the political oppression and the terror of Stalinism. In the minds of most Americans Communism was identified with Stalinism. There was no doubt about the ferocity of the Stalinist terror in the Soviet Union and also in the Eastern European countries that came under Soviet control. There was much genuine opposition to Communism as a cruel enemy of freedom.

The other element in postwar anti-Communism was the desire to keep as much of the world as possible free for capitalism and for penetration by American business. This anti-Communism continued for many years after the death of Stalin, after the nature of Communism as an international reality had become much more complex. We shall speak of that later. Here we want to point out that the end result of the American obsession with anti-Communism was our involvement in the Indochina war, and that it was that war which finally destroyed the foreign policy consensus. So much has been written about the war that we shall do no more than summarize its effect upon American thinking about foreign policy. We shall then indicate the effect of that war as a landmark in Christian thinking about war.

Vietnam a Watershed

American involvement in the Indochina war came to be perceived after about 1967 as a mistake. Our defeat there was the final lesson. Apart from the experience of defeat, a majority of our citizens came to realize that we had attempted to do what was impossible. We could not by military force prop up a government in South Vietnam that had neither moral nor political legitimacy against a nationalistic revolution. The mistake began when in the early '50s we gave strong support to the colonialism of the French and then took their place as foreign intruders in a nation that was fiercely nationalistic. Communism in North Vietnam and in the revolutionary movement in South Vietnam had become the instrument of this nationalism. We were in the position of trying to control history by bombing in a part of the world which we did not understand. Our leaders had assumed that a replay of American success in Europe was possible in Asia if we tried hard enough. We soon discovered that the conditions were entirely different.

How many Americans went beyond the judgment that the war was a mistake to the judgment that it was morally wrong, that it was an "unjust war," is difficult to say. It was certainly a conviction that had great strength in the student generation, in the churches, and among intellectuals. This moral judgment also came to be expressed by influential political leaders and in much of the liberal press. Official condemnation of the war by denominational bodies began in 1970 following quite remarkable antiwar witness and activity by unofficial religious groups. The Roman Catholic hierarchy in November 1971 declared that the war was an unjust war. This was the more remarkable because of the widespread Catholic anti-Communism and because of the superpatriotic position taken by such Catholic leaders as Cardinal Spellman a short time before. A Harris Poll in 1971 showed that 65 percent of the people regarded the war as morally wrong. One has to discount that figure to some extent because of the confusion that could have been present. People could judge something might be morally wrong and yet see it as the lesser evil. Even so, it is amazing how widespread this moral rejection of the war was even while our nation was still fighting.

The judgment that the war was a mistake took two forms. One was along the lines already mentioned. But there were many other people who believed that it was a mistake unless we were willing to go all out to win. They advised the invasion of North Vietnam or the use of bombs, perhaps nuclear bombs, to lay North Vietnam waste, to bomb it "into the stone age." Destructive as our bombing actually was, we did not invade North Vietnam or resort to nuclear attack. The failure to do this was regarded as the error and not that our cause was either morally wrong or politically self-defeating.

These responses to the war have led to a deep disillusionment about the effects of our policies based upon the previous consensus. A mixture of shame and frustration has caused a national trauma. Our nation had never been defeated before in war and we had been so recently on top of the world. Revelations of CIA operations in Chile and elsewhere and especially of assassination plots against foreign leaders have increased the sense of shame. Whatever be the right road, it is widely felt that we were on the wrong one. There is much talk of neo-isolationism, but generally those who opposed the war in Indochina because it was wrong and who call for "no more Vietnams" are the very people who are most concerned about peace in the world. They want to strengthen multilateral institutions, and to overcome economic injustice between nations. People who may seem to be isolationists from a strongly nationalistic or politically rightist point of view have seldom been averse to America's throwing its weight around in the world unilaterally.

The Indochina war was a landmark in American Christian thinking about war. For the first time on a large scale Christians in this country used the traditional distinction in Christian ethics between just and unjust wars to declare that a particular war was unjust even while it was being fought by our nation. There has developed widespread support for what we now call "selective conscientious objectors" to military service in that particular war. An intensive commitment to absolute pacifism has also emerged among a smaller group. Most of those who took these positions regarded the war as unjust because its objectives were unjust and because the methods of conducting it were unjust. The use of American military power to impose the American will on these countries in Indochina and especially to use it to support the oppressive and cruel regime in Saigon was regarded as wrong. Even clearer was the moral rejection of the means used, and especially the horrendous bombing, for years, of the people and the land in both North and South Vietnam, in Laos, and in Cambodia. There was wide agreement that this bombing was disproportionate in its destructive effects in relation to its objectives. Disproportionate is a bloodless word for a horribly bloody reality. The comment by the American major that we destroyed a village in order to save it seemed to apply to the war as a whole, whatever one may have thought of the original American purpose. It was also widely held that particular acts in the war were immoral in themselves because they did not discriminate between combatants and noncombatants. There was bombing from the air with napalm of large free-fire zones that were known to contain many villages, and the destruction of cities in North Vietnam especially. There were atrocities such as the indiscriminate killing at My Lai, and the torture and killing of people who were captured either as war prisoners or as suspected Viet Cong. The latter things were done on a large scale by the South Vietnamese with the cooperation of Americans in what were called programs of "pacification." These were the kinds of atrocities that caused Christians and others to regard the war as immoral and unjust in the means that were used by our side.

The effect of all of this has been that many Christians, whether they are absolute pacifists or not, have concluded that there is one type of war, the type in which our government may be most tempted to engage, which is morally out-of-bounds. We refer to wars of ideological intervention in the internal conflicts of other countries. This is not suggested as an inflexible law to be applied to all future unforeseen situations but it is presented as an important guide for future policy.

We recognize that there might be occasions for a nation to use limited military force, preferably under some kind of multilateral auspices, to deliver the people of another nation from either hopeless anarchy that is destroying them or from the genocidal brutality of an oppressive government. Who knows what combination of circumstances might confront a nation with some obligation to rescue others? And yet probably under present conditions efforts along this line most often would be counterproductive. Moreover, it would be especially difficult for the United States to engage in them without appearing to be imperialist in intention. One case that may stump those who seek to establish absolute laws of nonintervention was the action of Israel in rescuing hostages in the Uganda airport. That may well have been justified. What must be most guarded against is military intervention to impose the self-serving will of a strong nation on weak nations. We apply this principle both to the American intervention in Indochina and the Soviet intervention in Czechoslovakia in 1968.

BEYOND THE COLD WAR

An essential element in the postwar consensus now proves to be inadequate as a guide for policy. Most American decisions in foreign policy were seen in the context of the cold war between East and West, between the Communist nations and what was generally called "the free world." The free world was not and is not made up only of nations with free political institutions. It was anti-Communist but it included and includes many nations under rightist dictatorships. The United States has been the dominant power in the free world. It has used that power to counteract subversion from the left in many countries, to protect nations by a policy of deterrence against possible attack as in the case of Western

Europe, and to prevent by military action what was believed to be aggression against a nation with which we were allied. This last was true of the Korean war though that war became a matter of great controversy when our forces crossed the 38th parallel. That was also true of the war in Indochina according to official interpretations, but contrary to those interpretations this was a case of interference in a civil war in Vietnam.

It is our contention that the cold war as such belongs to the past, though the rivalry and the mutual suspicion between the United States and the Soviet Union still exists. This rivalry is not primarily a conflict about Communism but a conflict between two imperial nuclear powers, each able to destroy the other. The ideological conflict between the United States and Soviet Communism has left a deposit of misunderstanding. A curtain divides the two nations behind which the view that each has of the other is rigidly stereotyped. The Communist dictatorship supported by old Russian forms of secrecy and political controls shrouds its aims and plans in mystery. In the case of the United States its aims and plans are the subject of intensive public discussion. This difference, combined with a residue of the old obsessive anti-Communism, lies back of much of the fear of Soviet intentions in this country.

Why do we say that the cold war belongs to the past? The main reason is that the international Communist bloc has been shattered. Even so, the assumption that the take-over of territory by any Communist country would strengthen international Communism led us into the Indochina war. Even American security was believed to be at stake, for, as many assumed, if we did not stop the Communists in Indochina, we might have to do so nearer California. When there was an international Communist monolith it was not strange that the free world felt threatened from both Asia and Eastern

Europe at the same time. One of the ironies of the Indochina war was that our attacks on North Vietnam weakened a nationalistic Communist nation which has been determined to be free from control by either China or the Soviet Union. Thus we were weakening a nation that was a hindrance to whatever expansion we may have feared from either of the two great Communist powers. The split between the Soviet Union and China profoundly changed the world. It has largely removed the fear that what appeared to be a shrinking free world would be overwhelmed by international Communism.

The first break in the Communist bloc was the split between Tito's Yugoslavia and Stalinist Russia in 1948. We should now think of the broad spectrum among Communist nations ranging from North Korea, which seems to be the most closed of Communist nations at one end, to Poland, Hungary, and Yugoslavia at the other end. Beyond this spectrum among Communist regimes there is the more liberal type of Communism which has great power in Italy, and similar Communist movements in other Western European countries, including France. Yugoslavia has more cultural freedom and more freedom in economic life than the Soviet Union and it is much more open to the outside world. It is clamping down on political dissent in ways that cause anxiety among many of its friends who have admired its more liberal form of Communism. This may be in part a result of the precariousness of its national unity and the fear of Soviet undoing of the achievements of Tito after his death.

Hungary is often regarded as the most free internally of the Communist countries, but it preserves this freedom by following the Soviet Union in matters of foreign policy. It is indeed remarkable that twenty years after the failure of the Hungarian revolution in 1956, János Kádár has unobtrusively been successful in leading his country to so many of the objectives of that revolution. It is quite open to Western influences, and there is much freedom for travel in and out of the country. In 1976 the Manchester *Guardian* could report from Hungary the following about the Kádár regime: "He has worked hard at reconciliation, and restored a large measure of humanity and sense of relaxation to a society that was almost broken by the cruel rigidity of the Rakosci regime. The lessons of the 1956 uprising have not been forgotten. There are few Hungarians who do not argue that Kadar has consistently worked to find a balance between human rights and basic social needs. They accept the inevitability of Soviet troop presence. But far from being cowed by it they argue that Kadar has finely calculated Hungary's strategic importance to Russia and has won for himself a great deal of freedom for domestic affairs."[1]

Poland has had various periods of relative freedom and repression. Today there is considerable relaxation favorable to cultural freedom. Relations with the West are at a high point. West Germany's acceptance in principle of the Oder and Neisse rivers as the western boundary of Poland has made for better German-Polish relations. There has been one constant factor in Poland that has made it unique among Communist states. That is the power of the Roman Catholic Church which the government has never been able to crack because of its continuing hold upon the Polish people.

Czechoslovakia internally under the auspices of the Communist Party became for a short time the most free of all Communist countries. We remember how its efforts to develop a new model of Communism and to gain independence of the Soviet Union were stamped out by Russian tanks. The courageous "Charter 77" protesters show how much the commitment to a humanistic Communism is still alive. It would probably take no more than a change in Soviet policy to enable it to be dominant. No one knows when this may come, for the Soviet leaders are fearful both of the contagion of new ideas that threatens their own system and of Czechoslovakia as a possible weak spot in the line of military defense against the West.

It is a mark of the complexity of Communism in Eastern Europe that Romania has succeeded in gaining considerable political and economic freedom from the Soviet Union and is a favorite of the United States. Yet it remains one of the more repressive Eastern countries in its domestic policy.

In the Soviet Union itself the changes that have come are far less than we hoped for at the time of Stalin's death. There has been much erosion among the people of commitment to the Marxist-Leninist ideology though the socialistic institutions are taken for granted.[2] Repression of political dissent and of intellectuals who become visible in their independence still remains. In spite of this there is a great deal of intellectual ferment just below and just above the surface. The government makes an example of a few independent spirits and sends them to prison or to mental hospitals. But they are not shot as would have been the case in the days of Stalin. The tragic predicament of the Russian who does have an independent spirit is great. Alexander Solzhenitsyn was allowed to go into exile with his family and his papers. That was a gain. Andrei Sakharov remains a visible critic of the regime, and his prestige protects him from prison and from being completely muzzled. The best thing we can say about the Soviet Union in this context is that the all-pervasive terror of Stalin no longer exists and the average citizen no longer lives in fear.

How far is this continued repression in the Soviet Union a Russian holdover from habits of repression under czarist regimes and how far is it a mark of Communism? The answer may be that Communism, at least from an American or Western point of view, had a poor start in Russia because of its lack of experience of political or cultural freedom. One can only speculate as to what might have happened if Communism had come first, as Marx himself expected, in an advanced capitalistic country with democratic institutions. Revolutions are generally violent and involve harsh dealings with opponents. But decades of repression might have been avoided if there had been habits and institutions of freedom.

There is much debate in this country about Soviet intentions in the buildup of its military power. Fear of American power against the background of the furious anti-Communism of which there was so much in our past is one reason for it. We see this continuing on the American right in the strong attacks on détente. In Russian memory the American military presence in Siberia soon after the Russian revolution remains a symbol of the long-standing anti-Soviet stance of the United States, even though this small American military expedition in Siberia was not intended as a threat to the revolution but was rather an effort to deal with problems arising out of the First World War. George Kennan discusses this in his book *Russia and the West Under Lenin and Stalin* (Little, Brown & Company, Inc., 1961), Ch. 8. The facts were very complicated, involving German prisoners, a group of pro-Ally Czechs and the desire to forestall a movement of Japanese into the area. This American operation became confused in the minds of people, especially Russians, with British aid to White Russians under Admiral Kolchak, who was fighting the revolutionary government. Kennan says of the Allied policy in Russia in general: "Never, surely have countries contrived to show themselves at their worst as did the Allies in Russia from 1917 to 1920" (p. 117). American policies after the revolution were not conducive to the development of mutual trust between the United States and the Soviet Union even at a much later period. The United States did not recognize the Soviet government until fifteen years after the revolution. Memory of this background is important as we think today about the reasons why the Soviet Union is still influenced by fear of our power.

There are two recent books by perceptive American journalists who have represented *The New York Times* and *The Washington Post* respectively in the Soviet Union. *The Russians*[3] by Hedrick Smith and *Russia*[4] by Robert G. Kaiser give similar pictures of Russian institutions and of the Russian people. They say the same thing about a major motive underlying the Russian military buildup. Smith puts it in this way: "Like the czars before them, Soviet leaders are driven by a burning sense of inferiority and a determination to overcome Russia's historic backwardness. . . . It is impossible to exaggerate the gnawing inferiority complex as a clue to Russian motivation in relations with the West today."[5] He relates this to Soviet concern about nuclear might and to the fact that military technology is seen as a part of technological growth in general. Kaiser enlarges on the same theme: "I don't think that the words 'aggressive' or 'expansionist' adequately describe Soviet behavior in international affairs since future historians, I think, will have to conclude that during this period, it was the United States, not the Soviet Union, which was most prone to misjudge its true interests and to take questionable risks by using military force in international disputes. The Russians have behaved like people who want to be taken seriously on the world stage, who crave recognition as the second and co-equal superpower. Their eagerness for status and influence is troublesome, sometimes dangerous, but less worrisome than an actively aggressive and expansionist Soviet policy would be."[6]

A nation whose presidents have said so often that it must be "first" should have some understanding of this motivation.

The Soviet Union has ceased to be a revolutionary power giving world revolution a high priority. It uses its influence with foreign Communist parties and revolutionary movements to secure their usefulness to Soviet interests as a great power. The picture of the Soviet Union preparing for a final strike against the United States as the chief obstacle to Communism in the world is a common American nightmare. It was given popular currency in part because Khrushchev, whose mind was formed by Marxist-Leninism, said that the Russians would "bury us." He meant that the success of Communism would overwhelm us. Those words suggest a statement in *The Communist Manifesto,* written in 1848, that the failure of capitalism would make the bourgeoisie their own gravediggers preceding the victory of the proletariat. Khrushchev knew very well that a nuclear war would be the end of the hopes of both sides.

Someone in our government should have plans to meet the worst that might happen. But foreign policy should not be based on the expectation of the most irrational Soviet behavior possible. Such policy might have the effect of self-fulfilling prophecy. There is a strong tendency in our Pentagon to stress Soviet intentions. There is a Russian Pentagon that probably does the same in regard to the United States. A troublesome difference is that while our Pentagon may be in open debate with other units of our government and with many representatives of the public, no one knows about the content of the debates in the Soviet government. There are only speculations about them based on who seem to be the top men in the politburo at a given time. We can understand why this element of mystery in the Kremlin worries Americans. This is sufficient reason for not engaging in all-out unilateral disarmament but rather for taking unilateral steps in the reduction of arms in the hope that they may be reciprocated. In the meantime it is well to reflect on our own capacity to destroy the Soviet Union many times over. We should also realize that since the Second World War we have used more violence, dropped more bombs on people than all other countries in the world put together. Others need reassurance as well as ourselves.

There is a final suggestion that we want to make about American policy in relation to the tension between Communist and non-Communist nations. Far too often our policy has been to drive nations which show signs of being influenced by Marxism or Communism together into the same camp. Our dealing with Yugoslavia after 1948 is an exception to this, and more recently we seem to have been encouraging Romania in its relative independence. Late in the day we seized upon the conflict between China and the Soviet Union to encourage the former as a balancing power in relation to the Soviet Union. But in other contexts we have not done this. Cuba is the worst case. We forced Cuba to become completely dependent on the Soviet Union. Was not the Cuban action in Angola quite likely a consequence of this? Would not recent history have been quite different if we had helped Castro's revolution to succeed? We tried to strangle it and failed. We could not have had a worse result if we had taken the opposite course. How far was our action influenced by Cuban exiles in America? Castro allowed his chief opponents to emigrate to Miami instead of forcing them to stay in Cuba. But we allowed this to become a chief cause of hostility toward Castro, which in some segments of public opinion became obsessive. It was easier for an American President to go to Peking than to Havana. We hope that this will change.

Each case is different. It might have been wiser to help Allende develop a new and different left-wing model in Chile. Few things could be worse than the present misery of Chile for which our government has considerable responsibility. What will be our relation with the new Vietnam? Will we treat it as we have treated Cuba for fifteen years? That would be a mistake so far as any influence we might have on the development of a more open type of Communist society is concerned. It would be dreadfully wrong, because we owe help to Vietnam to repair some of the destruction that we visited on the nation for no reason that now bears scrutiny. Our intervention in Angola in 1976 may well be another example of a mistaken policy in dealing with the internal struggles of emerging nations, not least because we intervened in cooperation with South Africa.

Our official lack of sympathy for the development of a more open and independent type of Communism in Western Europe is another example of the tendency to push all who have the Marxist or Communist infection into the same camp. Italian Communism is different in its philosophy and political direction and its spirit from Soviet Communism. Italians are so independent that it is a mistake to base policy on the assumption that in a crunch Italian Communists will prove to have an overriding loyalty to the Soviet Union. Policy based upon that assumption might help to create the very thing that is feared. Much more than official policy is involved; it is countless relationships between Americans and Italians. French Communism may be the same as Italian in this respect, but its history may cause one to be less confident about it. Western European Communism may be the most hopeful example of diversity within the broad Marxist-Communist movement. Communism will not go away. We can live with it best if there is diversity within it and if models of Communism develop that relate it in new and hopeful ways to democratic habits and democratic institutions.

BEYOND THE COUNTERREVOLUTIONARY POLICY

American anti-Communism caused us to become involved in a counterrevolutionary foreign policy on several continents. We found ourselves strong supporters or allies of rightist tyrannies that care nothing about the freedom we prize. At the same time they do little or nothing for the lower 50 to 80 percent of their populations. Our only tests for giving support have been whether or not governments were anti-Communist and whether the countries were open to penetration by American business, tests that have nothing to do with either freedom or justice. We have in mind such regimes as the following: Brazil, post-Allende Chile, President Thieu's South Vietnam, South Korea, Suharto's Indonesia. For several years the Greek regime of the colonels was our ally. Iran seems to be a special favorite today in spite of massive cruelty in dealing with dissenters. The government on Taiwan may do more for the people but it remains a police state and in spite of some ambiguities it remains a special ally. The present regime in the Philippines is another example. We could go on and cite such episodes as the CIA intervention to establish a rightist government in Guatemala. Our government cannot expect to support only democracies for reasons that we shall mention later. But the regimes we have cited have been especially cruel in suppressing dissent, and many of them have been notorious for their use of torture on political prisoners. Also, in some cases, the best-known ones being in Latin America, our government has trained and equipped the police and other operatives engaged in repression. There has also been complacent cooperation by both the American government and American business with racist regimes in South Africa and Rhodesia though official rhetoric has recently changed in favor of majority rule in those countries.

World politics as well as national politics make strange bedfellows. We cannot criticize our government for cooperating in many ways with governments of which it may disapprove. Our concern is that we have in many cases tried to prevent change. Where we might have exerted influence to prevent torture, for example, this has not been done. There has been a double standard with emphasis on instances of cruel repression on the left but with indifference toward similar or even worse practices on the right. One example of this is that we soon forgot the massacre of from five hundred thousand to a million people in a few weeks in Indonesia in 1965 because the victims were Communists or those suspected to be or framed as Communists. In this country this terrible event hardly caused a ripple.

American policymakers have justified their support of rightist regimes that may repel them as persons on two grounds. One is that they are not a part of the global Communist threat to the free world. They may be used in particular places to prevent the spread of Communism, and the wrongs they do affect only their own people or perhaps their immediate neighbors. This was understandable when there was such a thing as monolithic international Communism. Today we are not justified in making use of this excuse. Also, we have no right to assume that in a particular country we should seek to prevent the success of a leftist revolution whether or not it receives support from a Communist country. There has been an axiom to the effect that a Communist regime is the worst fate that can come to any country, worse than stagnation in poverty for generations, worse than continuing civil war, worse than a rightist tyranny. When have we seriously considered the nature of these alternatives? This is not an assumption for us to make for other countries. Yet it has been the moral justification for any efforts that we may have made to save a country from Communism.

The other rationalization of this policy has been that a rightist regime, however repressive, is believed to be less irreversible than a Communist regime. It lacks ideological coherence and has no base in the loyalty of a large segment of the people and it is often inefficient. A Communist regime, however, with its Marxist philosophy, its skill in indoctrination, and its economic programs for most of the population is said to be irreversible.

There is some truth in this view. It is more likely that a country like Brazil or Chile may change regimes than it is that this would happen in China or Cuba. And such a change might be in the direction of more pluralism or openness or even democratic freedoms. This remains speculative. However, Communist societies also change even if their regimes are not displaced. In the meantime they do deal with problems of justice that the rightist regimes generally neglect. If the United States had been successful in enabling the Nationalist forces of Chiang Kai-shek to destroy Communism in China, what moral satisfaction could we take today? Almost certainly it would have meant that the Chinese people would still be in their poverty, and they might have been thrown back into an endless civil war and even into anarchy.

It is both the irony and the tragedy of American history that our nation, begun in revolution and for generations inspiring most of the world with ideals of freedom, should today become an obstacle to forms of revolutionary change that are different from ours. We should have had more humility as we have faced the vast social upheavals within which various forms of Marxism have been agents of change. Hannah Arendt in her illuminating book *On Revolution* cites the American Revolution as the most successful of revolutions, and one of the reasons for this success is that "it occurred in a country that knew nothing of mass poverty and among a people who had a widespread experience of self-government."[7] This is true even though there was large-scale poverty among blacks and native Americans who were outside the community of white citizens who made the revolution and established the new nation. It should give us pause when we attempt to control those situations in which people are struggling against the poverty of centuries and in which they have not had the advantage that comes from experience in self-government. There may not be an alternative available to people in many other situations that is in line with our political vision or our experience.

Professor Brzezinski in an article already quoted warns that the United States may become isolated in a hostile world. It has been wedded to the ideal of liberty, whereas "the idea of equality is increasingly the underlying mood and the felt aspiration in an increasingly congested world, and it is more often than not first expressed by intellectuals." That is a most helpful statement of our situation, but it might be better to avoid stating the problem in terms of an abstract egalitarianism. The missing element in the American view of social change in the world may better be identified as the emphasis upon the need for social justice. Even a significant leap toward social justice may be more within reach than equality, though justice should always be under the pull of the idea of equality. The struggle against desperate inequalities is in many nations the immediate agenda. The United States should put this item higher on its own agenda since our prevalent affluence is shadowed by the poverty of more than twenty-five million people. Fresh thinking is needed about the relation between liberty and justice while keeping the emphasis on both. A one-sided ideology that accents one and not the other is not good enough at home or abroad.

HUMAN RIGHTS AND THE DECLINE OF DEMOCRACY

We believe in a constitutional type of democracy that provides both for majority rule and for the protection of the rights of minorities and of individuals. We find it painful, therefore, that in so much of the world democracy is rejected out of hand. Without our being dogmatic about any particular case, it does seem that democratic institutions are not viable in many situations. Nations that have just gained freedom from colonial domination lack political experience to face the most acute social conflicts, be they ideological, economic, or tribal. We regret that American leaders sometimes use rhetoric that polarizes the world in terms of democratic and nondemocratic nations. When they do so they seem oblivious of our own government's strong support of nondemocratic regimes so long as they are on the right rather than on the left.

We should be more sympathetic concerning the difficulties which many nations have in establishing or preserving democracy. Many of them do not have in their traditions the experience and resources that have proved favorable to democratic institutions where they have developed with some success. There is something to be learned from a remarkable dialogue between Reinhold Niebuhr and Hans Morgenthau on this subject. Both of them in their writings have shown a profound belief in the desirability of democracy. One of the strongest arguments for democracy under modern conditions is found in Niebuhr's *The Children of Light and the Children of Darkness.* [8] Niebuhr says in his dialogue with Morgenthau: "You know, Morgenthau, I think that it is fantastic to regard democracy as a universal option for all people. That is as fantastic in its way as Communist dogma and utopianism." Later he repeats his famous sentence: "Man's capacity for justice makes democracy possible; man's inclination to injustice makes democracy necessary." He goes on to say that you cannot have justice without the consent of the governed but that this consent may not be possible everywhere. Morgenthau's response is that there are other conceptions of justice than those based on individualism; the "idea of service to the family or to the village community may be an incarnation of justice." He points out that our liberal conceptions of justice depend upon the experience of a number of European revolutions, "the Renaissance, the Reformation, the Enlightenment, the French revolution," and that "there is an almost insane disregard of historical conditioning of politics in our approach to Asia."[9] (Fortunately changes in India, Spain, and Portugal show that it is possible to move from an authoritarian regime toward democracy.)

There is some danger of developing a Western elitism that denies to people in other countries the possibility of finding their way to many elements of democracy, perhaps in institutional forms quite different from our own. Also there are values associated in our minds with democracy, for which we believe democracy to be the best protection. To these we should bear witness and we should encourage their adoption in any part of the world where we have influence. We should not be complacent about these values, and I am sure that no such complacency would represent either Niebuhr or Morgenthau. In what follows we shall spell out the meaning of three such values. American foreign policy without military intervention in the affairs of other nations should express our nation's concern about those values. In detail there will always be room for debate as to what policies are useful and what policies are counterproductive in this regard. But commitment to them should be expressed in any way possible by our nation in its relation with other nations.

The first value associated with democracy is the preservation of the dignity of the person over against the practice of so many nations of imprisoning dissenters without trial or of torturing them. The prevalence of torture is one of the most repellent realities in today's world. It degrades those who inflict it or consent to it and it violates the humanity of the victims. The international character of the methods of causing pain and suffering is startling as one reads accounts of torture in nation after nation. Regardless of what people may believe about democratic institutions, they are repelled when they know of this use of torture by their governments. Publicity about torture places governments on the moral defensive. Amnesty International is able to get into many situations and to keep the facts before that part of the world where there is still freedom for ideas and information to reverberate. Within countries where churches can do little to influence political structures, they can still keep pressures on governments in regard to this despicable practice.

A second value associated with democracy to which people should be committed is the right of conscience in the expression of faith and convictions. The situation in regard to this kind of freedom varies a great deal among countries that have no constitutional protection of the rights of the individual. Often people assert such rights even when they are not legally protected, and they are able to push doors open beyond expectations. This requires great courage and involves costly struggles. We have referred to the intellectual ferment just below and just above the surface in the Soviet Union. There is an unpublished literature that is passed around from person to person. In some countries religious freedom, even when its external expression is limited, can be taken and used. The presence of a church that has a strong structure and faithful members often enables people to push out those limits to freedom. The record of churches as defenders of the human rights of all people, not only of their own members, in many countries is one of the bright chapters in church history. Organized religion, organized science, and organizations of jurists are powers that governments are often forced to respect. Sometimes the work of artists who have visions that transcend the limits imposed by political power can be seen or heard when other free expressions of the spirit are restricted. There is something basic in our humanity that is not universally recognized but that in spite of the greatest obstacles keeps demanding freedom of expression for mind and conscience. When Christians say, "We must obey God rather than men," they are making that demand for themselves and preparing the way for others to make it.

A third value is the overcoming of discrimination against people anywhere on account of race or sex. There are strong forces working for this value even in nations that have no democratic protections of freedom. To be charged with racism is to be disgraced in a large part of the world even when there may be some inconsistency among those who make the charges, for they may be guilty of some form of reverse racism. Sexism may not be regarded as disgraceful in as wide circles but we have not yet seen what the pressures of women on the institutions, habits, and attitudes of male chauvinism can do to loosen up oppressive patterns. It is to be hoped that this new force, the growing self-consciousness of women, may break restrictive patterns far beyond those related to sex. The extraordinary joint intervention in the summer of 1976 of Catholic and Protestant women for the sake of peace in the unending bloody conflict in Northern Ireland is an example of the kind of influence women can have in the broader political area. Anti-Semitism is less universally understood or rejected than is white racism. But there are large and important areas where it too is seen as a disgrace, as an expression of an ancient evil related to the horrors of Nazism.

We do not claim that it will be easy to strike blows against these forms of discrimination, but the whole continent of Africa is on fire with hatred of white racism. The pressures on oppressive white racist governments increase daily. As we write, there seems to be a change in American policy in relation to the racist governments in South Africa and Rhodesia, but this is only a precarious beginning. Related to this may surface one of the great struggles in contemporary American politics in the years immediately ahead. One form that it may take may be a struggle against any tendency to use American military power on the side of white governments against black majorities for the sake of American economic interests.

China may well raise the most profound issues concerning the claims of justice and freedom. Since the opening of China to Westerners in recent years, the reports from China have generally been favorable and even enthusiastic. Critics of this tendency are probably right in saying that many people are too uncritical and their reports are suggestive of a new utopianism. Present-day China does not have the concern for freedom of expression for the individual that we prize and that is in line with the second of the values mentioned above. This kind of individualism was certainly not present under recent anti-Communist regimes in China. It does not fit traditional Chinese culture. The contemporary emphasis on social cooperation and on communal life is as much Chinese as it is Communist.

The remarkable fact about China today is that it is the one country with most dehumanizing mass poverty which has overcome that poverty. People there no longer starve. China can be an example to us in bringing health care to the whole population both in cities and in rural areas. Also, the people of China have attained dignity as members of cooperating communities. Theirs is not an individualistic conception of dignity, but there is an approach to equality and to mutual aid that has its own high value. No longer is China a nation that is humiliated by Western domination. While it is passionately and pridefully nationalistic, it does not show signs of being aggressively militaristic. It has rounded out its territory and intends to do this, in time, in connection with Taiwan. It has limited itself to what both the Peking government and the Taiwan government agree to be the boundaries of China. To recognize this does not necessarily mean approval of particular actions, as in Tibet, but it does give ground for believing that China is not indefinitely expansionist. The nightmare of China as a threat to its Asian neighbors, which was partly responsible for our involvement in Indochina, no longer torments many Americans. Both the Chinese and the Russians do worry about the thousands of miles of border which they share.

We hope that China will find its own way to the spiritual and cultural freedom that is so precious to us, even though it may take different institutional forms. We cannot help questioning whether in the long run achievements of social justice are likely to survive without freedom to expose and criticize the abuses that generally distort the use of unchecked power. Mao Tsetung's conception of permanent revolution provides the frame for ways of checking power. It is more consistent with the Christian view of the human situation than the Leninist assumption that the revolution would bring about a utopia in which the state as a coercive institution would wither away. The recent "cultural revolution" took the form of exposing the bureaucracy and and shaking up leadership of the Party. It was the effect of Mao's own manipulation and of grass-roots popular initiatives. It involved extremist actions that Mao himself had to curtail. How such agents of change can be structured and also restrained in the future is an open question. Permanent revolution could come to mean little more than a succession of tumults followed by repression even if there is essential wisdom underlying the idea.

We believe that our attitude toward China should be controlled by a sense of the immensity of the problem of overcoming the injustices of the centuries. This caused a human upheaval of gigantic proportions. We cannot expect what comes out of it to fit the specifications of those of us who live in a vastly different situation and who are beneficiaries of earlier revolutions and of changes that have taken many generations. Humility before these upheavals is called for and gratitude for the considerable achievements in terms of justice and human dignity should dominate American attitudes toward China and influence the presuppositions of American policy. (For a different view of the significance of China, see the stimulating discussion of a comparison of Brazil and China as two models for Third World development in Peter Berger's *Pyramids of Sacrifice* [Basic Books, Inc., 1974], Ch. V.)

We conclude by returning to the emphasis given earlier. We need to preserve as large an area of the world as possible with freedom to circulate information and ideas, where cultural institutions can have autonomy, and where expressions of religious and ethical convictions are not limited by political intimidation or persecution. It would be disastrous if there were no country with a free press, or a free university, or a free church, no country where such international meetings as the assemblies of the World Council of Churches or the UN conferences on food, population, environment, "habitat," or the rights of women could be held with the chance for full publicity. This would be the case if such agencies as Amnesty International or the International Commission of Jurists were unable to investigate denials of human rights and make their findings known. The responsibility of nations that now have this freedom is not to try to impose their institutions on other nations. Rather it is to pursue foreign policies that encourage open societies while preserving and making use of their own freedom in trust for the whole world. In this way, information and ideas about what is happening to people everywhere can be known and become a force for change.

International Ethics
and Economic Privilege

THOSE WHO BENEFIT from any situation are not likely to recognize deficiencies in the system that treats them so well. Yet, economic statistics in the modern world make inequality so obvious that even our most stubborn prejudices are blasted away. Nine hundred million people with cash incomes of less than seventy-five dollars a year, subsist under conditions which World Bank president Robert McNamara has called "so deprived as to be below any rational definition of human decency."[1] Acutely hungry persons total about 460 million. When we add those who lack essential nutrients in their diet, and who therefore cannot function at full capacity, the UN Food and Agricultural Organization estimates that the number rises to between one and two billion.[2]

THE NATURE AND CONSEQUENCES OF ECONOMIC INEQUALITY

In areas inhabited by two thirds of the world's population the chief nutritional problem is malnutrition. In our country the number one nutritional problem is obesity. From 1972 to 1974, the average annual per capita grain consumption (both directly and indirectly, as in feeding cattle for meat) was 1,850 pounds in the United States and only 395 pounds in the developing countries. Annual per capita consumption of fossil fuels in 1970 was 246 kilograms for poorer countries and 4,420 kilograms for industrially developed countries.[3] The United States with about 6 percent of the world's population uses about 40 percent of the world's consumption of natural resources.

Furthermore, the gap between economically rich and poor nations has been widening. From 1960 to 1970 the average per capita income in developed countries increased 43 percent while the increase was only 27 percent in the Third World (the poorer preindustrial nations).[4] Those countries now sometimes referred to as the Fourth World (not only industrially undeveloped but lacking resources for development) will actually experience negative growth rates without extraordinary help. When income figures for the poor are so much lower to start with, it takes a considerably higher percentage increase before they begin to catch up. Poorer nations are in the position of a bicycle rider trying to overtake the driver of a racing car. Even though both are moving ahead, the distance between them becomes steadily greater. Those nations which have become stronger have important advantages in future competition. As Robert Lichtman put it, "It is as though after every race the runners were permitted to start again from the position in which they found themselves at the termination of the previous race."[5]

Inequality between nations may be partly the responsibility of persons in the developing world. Some leaders have acted unwisely or perpetrated injustices on their own people. Customary habits do sometimes keep production lower. But there are other major causes that the poor nations can do little about. We inherited our own head start from the work of previous generations. We have had unusual natural and political advantages. These advantages cannot be duplicated by many of the poorer nations.

In addition, more powerful nations have often enforced conditions that exploited disadvantaged areas. Under imperialist controls, rich nations shaped the economies of colonial areas to maximize their own profits. For example, we bought raw materials from less developed countries, but by our tariff arrangements we enforced our monopoly of more profitable types of manufactured goods. We built our higher living standards partly on low wages and low selling prices in the mines and plantations of the Third World. Our prosperity has to a great extent depended on the poverty of others. In a world of limited resources, one person's wealth inevitably becomes another person's poverty. The current "affluence explosion" in our part of the world is consuming global resources that could be directed to greater and more elemental human needs. Part of the social costs of the second car in our garages, and of the trailer and boat behind the car is lack of housing and transportation in poorer nations.

Existing international inequalities become a major cause of war. Enclaves of plenty in an environment of poverty understandably stimulate hostile responses against the degradation and injustice of the situation. When the anger of the oppressed explodes into widespread violence, we may have such a time of terrorism, revolution, and war as humankind has never before experienced. Even more ominous, perhaps, is the prospect of the poor of the earth being used as pawns in a game of power politics between the great powers. As wealthy nations back different factions in the developing world, the sponsoring powers also confront each other with the full threat of their military might. There can be no lasting peace without justice in the redistribution of resources. Justice delayed is a major cause of insurrection. The disposition of the privileged to cling to their disproportionate wealth becomes a chronic threat to peace.

Turmoil and conflict will be intensified as essential resources near exhaustion. Even the invention of substitutes for some presently scarce items cannot be a permanent solution. Eventually some of the resources necessary for further invention will have disappeared. As indicated above, 6 percent of the earth's population is now absorbing approximately 40 percent of the natural resources used in any given period. If the other 94 percent of the world's population is to match that living standard, the earth will the sooner be left an uninhabited and mined-out planet spinning through space. At the same time, industrial exploitation of resources fills up the earth's capacity to absorb pollutants and waste. Over wide areas there is already a serious strain on air and rivers due to "the sheer scale of effluents to be disposed of and materials to be junked—1900 pounds per person per year for instance in the United States."[6] As life-support systems approach extinction, conflict over access to what remains can be expected to become more bitter.

THE ETHICS OF PRIVILEGE AND NEED

There is a strong theological and ethical basis for the reversal of cultural trends which our society has exhibited. The material world belongs to God who created it and who has purposes for it (Lev. 25:23; Ps. 24:1). Ours can never be an absolute asceticism, in the sense of claiming that material things are evil. Instead, material things are the good gifts of God. Economic activity has important religious significance. Economic production and consumption can contribute to the realization of the purposes of God in material creation. God intends that material goods should contribute to the actualization of the highest potentialities of persons. Every person, therefore, is to have opportunity for access to God's creation. In all these respects in which material things contribute to personal fulfillment, God wants each of his children to travel first class—but that includes those in the far reaches of the earth and in future generations also.

One test for any economy is what happens to the least fortunate or the most disadvantaged group served by it. The Christian conscience cannot be satisfied with any unjust discrimination in the distribution of available goods and services. This does not necessarily mean that resources are to be distributed equally. Since different people have different needs, they have somewhat different claims to whatever is necessary to meet their legitimate requirements. For example, whenever we provide for a chronically ill person with heavy medical bills only the same income as is received by healthy citizens, we effectively limit the sickly citizen's access to the nonmedical resources that others can afford to buy. The guideline is not exact statistical equality in income or material goods, but rather equality of opportunity. Provided that they are willing to carry their just share of productive work, all people are entitled to similar access to resources as needed. But such equal opportunity to satisfy genuine needs is repeatedly violated by present patterns of distribution. Existing inequalities have become so great and have so little relationship to need, that they no longer allow equal opportunity to the poor.

The test of equal opportunity applies not only within nations but also between nations. When any nation unjustly holds onto more than its rightful share of available wealth, others are deprived of similar access to the resources of God's earth. One implication of this was well stated by Charles Birch to the 1975 Nairobi meeting of the World Council of Churches, "According to the criterion of justice, any country would be overdeveloped whose standard of living was beyond the capacity of the world to generate for all its peoples."

Another way of putting this is to say that it is the intention of God that economic processes shall meet human need to the fullest possible extent. The message of the parable of the good Samaritan is that need anywhere constitutes a claim on resources everywhere. The existence of important need should be a sufficient stimulus to release the neighborly response of service. The Deuteronomic code took seriously the needs of the poor (Deut. 15:7–8). The prophets vigorously condemned those who "trample upon the poor" (Amos 2:6–7; 5:11–12; Isa. 3:14–15; 58:1–7). Jesus sternly rebuked those who "devour widows' houses" (Mark 12:40; Luke 20:47).

The prophetic tradition in the Bible is especially severe in its judgment on the rich and the powerful. They have the resources to meet need. Withholding those resources is grievous sin to be severely punished. The Apocrypha puts this in a way that is still today both sociologically and morally accurate. "Scanty fare is the living of the poor; the man who deprives them of it is a murderous man. The man who takes away his neighbor's living murders him." (Ecclus. 34:21–22, Goodspeed translation.) When those of us in the more fortunate parts of the world simply maintain the high standard of living to which we have typically aspired, we condemn others to starvation. Is this not as certain a source of death as shooting? We prosecute those who incite to riot or who explode terroristic bombs. We excuse or even honor those who most conspicuously divert wealth from the poor to their own consumption.

If we take seriously the doctrine of creation and the sovereignty of God, we cannot use and dispose of our property as we see fit. We are always to beware of the pride of possession (Deut. 8:11–18). It is not ours to do what we wish with what we "own." God alone is the ultimate owner of the wealth of the world. We are to act as stewards, managing the resources of the earth according to the purposes of God. An unavoidable test of our devotion to God is how we use the forests and factories and uranium deposits, which have come under our stewardship, to serve human need.

With all our temptations to excessive compromise, we are bound to remember the radical claims of love which we are to approximate as closely as possible under existing limiting circumstances. Christian love moves beyond mutuality. It gives priority to the neighbor's needs. It is all-inclusive in its scope, and it is willing to make sacrifices if necessary. With the same overflowing and nondiscriminatory goodwill with which God loves us, so are we to love others (I John 4:7–12). To be sure, mixed motives operate in all of us and the imperfections of our love limit what is socially possible. Furthermore, the ambiguities of the human situation require accommodations. To realize one value for one group may mean the denial of other values to other groups. To maintain peace for one's own country may allow the loss of freedom for other peoples. Yet our guideline still remains the fullest possible expression of the inclusively other-regarding spirit of love. History makes it clear that if we ignore the requirements of goodwill and mutual regard, all humankind faces irreversible disaster. That fact becomes a call to an imaginative, adventurous, innovative action.

The comparative claims of the near neighbor and the far neighbor are a recurring issue in Christian ethics. Is it legitimate to give first claim on our resources to our own children or to the citizens of our own country? Conventional wisdom holds that "charity begins at home," but it is increasingly hard to maintain this and at the same time follow the guideline that resources are to be used at the point of greatest need. We can scarcely argue for our right to resources because of the skill or hard work of our ancestors. Since we did not choose our grandparents, we deserve no credit for a wise choice. Many other geographical and historical factors, in addition to skill and labor, were involved in past productivity. Furthermore, a great many of the world's poor receive scant returns, although they are working a great deal harder than those of us who have machines and social legislation.

Some resources can be used more efficiently near at hand. But this argument also loses its force as resources can now more easily be transferred, for example, by bank checks or cargo planes. Or it may be claimed that parents have a particular vocation to care for their own children. But why should Americans be able to fulfill that vocation in ways that are denied to African parents? In view of all these qualifications, there is surprisingly little to be said for using our wealth first for those closest to us. Or to put it another way, "our own" now must include every member of the human family. When a child anywhere suffers from malnutrition, it is as though my child were undernourished. Charity may begin at home, but it does not end there. Karl Barth said of the Christian, "As he holds his near neighbors with the one hand, he reaches out to the distant with the other."[7]

Such action in response to need is a condition for the most intimate relationship with God (Matt. 25:31–46). To stand close to God, we must also stand close to the hungry and needy, because that is where God is standing. Karl Barth said it this way, "God always takes His stand unconditionally and passionately on this side [the side of the poor and oppressed] and on this side alone: against the lofty and on behalf of the lowly; against those who already enjoy right and privilege and on behalf of those who are denied it."[8] If we claim to believe in God, we cannot avoid serving the poor. José Míguez-Bonino, a theological voice from the Third World, is quite orthodox in saying, "There cannot be, in the nature of the case, a *believing* disobedience—unless it is the 'dead faith' of which James speaks, and which 'profits nothing' "[9] (James 2:15–17).

The liberation theologians rightly insist that spiritual growth for the rich requires disposing of part of their wealth to the poor. Gustavo Gutiérrez said, "One loves the oppressors by liberating them from their inhuman condition as oppressors."[10] The poor lack the opportunities for social and spiritual growth that a better material base could provide. The rich, along with decline in sensitivity to suffering, experience the erosion of morality and spiritual development. Their deadly sins become pride, rationalization, and exploitation. While starvation and affluence coexist, both rich and poor live in an enervating environment.

Those of us who are the rich of the earth need to meditate long on I John 3:17, "If any one has the world's goods and sees his brother in need, yet closes his heart against him, how does God's love abide in him?" In the words of Jesus, we are like a camel trying to get through a needle's eye (Matt. 19:23–24; Mark 10:25). America's number one spiritual problem may well be, "How can a rich man enter the Kingdom of Heaven?"

THE FORMS AND LIMITS OF ECONOMIC ASSISTANCE

Rich nations face similar humanitarian claims for a reversal of past policy. Traditional economic nationalism made the welfare of the rest of the world a secondary consideration. Insofar as nationalism became imperialism, it even made the exploitation of the rest of the world a primary purpose. In the light of the ethics we profess, development and liberation of the poorer nations deserve at least equal billing with our own welfare.

Several forms of economic assistance need to be built into our foreign policy. One of these is to facilitate trade which is profitable to the Third World. The price that consumers in the United States are willing to pay for coffee is related to the rate of general economic progress of the coffee-producing countries. The principal source of capital for developing nations is trade, not direct grants of aid. To earn foreign exchange by exports ordinarily has advantages over paying interest on loans from abroad. Policies that reduce the prices at which developing nations can sell their exports take away with one hand the economic assistance we give with the other. Desirable changes in trade policies will be further discussed in the next chapter.

Another important element in lifting the status of the dispossessed is population control. The more babies to be fed and the more elderly people to be housed, the greater will be the demands on available resources. In 1974, at the UN Bucharest conference on population, it was predicted that the earth's population would double within thirty years if growth rates were not checked.

Some regions of the world face a less critical pressure on their land area than others. But even these countries face critical pressures on housing, sanitation, transportation, and other agricultural and industrial services necessary to develop their land. We all live in one world in which changes in the total global population change the situation for all regions of the earth. It is understandable that especially needy nations should feel that economic growth should be given such a high priority as to eclipse population control. They are right to challenge our contention that it is impossible to provide the essential needs for a sizable world population so long as we insist on consuming more than we need and so long as we spend as much as we do on armaments. But they are wrong in suggesting that development does not require stabilization of population. Where the marginal product of an additional worker is low—or even nonexistent—his or her contribution is outweighed by the cost of services to that worker, like health, education, and transport. Under generally prevailing conditions, more children require more resources even to maintain the present level of subsistence. Robert McNamara has observed, "A treadmill economy tends to emerge, in which the total national effort will exhaust itself by running faster and faster merely to stand still."[11]

Ansley J. Coale's research indicated that if a typically undeveloped country reduced its fertility by 50 percent in a period of 25 years, it could double the income per consumer in 60 years and triple it in 90 years. After 150 years, the average income would be 6 times as great as it would have been had the original population growth remained unchanged.[12]

Not only does population control contribute to development, but the reverse is also true. As standards of living go up, experience indicates that the birthrate tends to decline. A greater prospect of continuing security makes many children unnecessary as a kind of "old age insurance" to provide for elderly parents. A higher level of economic expectations, including more employment opportunities and status for women, contributes to smaller family size. The poorer nations have a right to stabilize their population in the same way that industrialized nations did—by making social and economic gains.

It is not a question of population stabilization or economic development. Rather, it is a matter of "both/and." The two objectives reinforce each other. Motivation must be provided by socioeconomic development, while strong family-planning programs are also made available. For maximum effectiveness, economic assistance programs must include both elements.

We wish now to concentrate on a third form of economic aid, namely, governmental assistance through technical services and capital grants or loans. The ethical considerations already discussed provide a strong drive toward some sort of sharing of these resources. There are also a number of cold, hard realities of economic life which point in the same direction. In the first place, there can be no adequate rise in standard of living for the poor of the world without sufficient capital to provide the equipment and support facilities necessary to increase productivity.

Secondly, this capital can come from either inside or outside the developing country. If it is to be generated internally, consumption standards must be sufficiently depressed to provide the surplus necessary for improving the productive sector of the economy. Totalitarian political controls become necessary to impose such limitations on consumer goods. By withholding larger amounts of outside aid, we become partly responsible for the authoritarianism that then becomes necessary.

As a third practical consideration, capital from outside a developing country can be obtained either from philanthropy, private business investment, or government funds. Philanthropy from individuals, churches, or foundations cannot come near providing the amount of capital needed. To depend on business investments from abroad understandably raises questions in receiving nations about draining off profits and fear of foreign control over their economy. Besides, many of the essentials for development, such as irrigation, highways, river and harbor improvement, or basic education, do not normally return a profit to investors and are not therefore attractive as business ventures. The limitations of philanthropy and private investment leave no alternative but to provide supplementary government funds for economic assistance from the industrialized nations.

A fourth fact is that development becomes a more

complex and difficult problem than we have often realized. Economic justice now requires a greater understanding of developing nations and more extensive forms of service than we have heretofore been willing to give. Vast infrastructures of economic growth include items like schools, transportation, and communication networks. Personal attitudes and social customs must sometimes be altered. Revolutionary political and social changes may be required if the assistance is to be effective.

The magnitude of the upsetting worldwide change involved is suggested in a fifth compelling reality. We will not close the gap between rich and poor nations without lowering the material consumption of rich nations. As already indicated there are limits to the physical resources of a finite planet. Our past efforts to share wealth painlessly relied on increasing the size of the production pie. Then both the small pieces and the large pieces could simultaneously get bigger. That was never a sufficient approach. Now it is becoming impossible. As the ingredients for a larger pie become more scarce—and as we realize that we are getting indigestion from our oversized piece—there is no rational and moral alternative to cutting our share smaller so that others may have an equal opportunity for nourishment.

Basic disagreements between proponents and opponents of economic assistance arise about how serious the situation is and how sacrificial we should be in meeting it. These central issues are too seldom faced. Arguments popularly used against economic assistance repeatedly turn out not to be arguments against foreign aid as such. Illustrations of inefficiency, waste, pauperization, or corruption do not challenge the inherent nature of the program. They are arguments only against particular types of assistance programs or the manner in which they are administered. It needs to be more widely understood that such criticisms do not support the case for abandoning economic assistance, but only for improving it. Creative economic assistance programs are often blocked by such arguments that apply only to weak programs. Those who participate in this kind of misleading propaganda must finally face the judgment, "I was hungry and you gave me no food, I was thirsty and you gave me no drink" (Matt. 25:42).

Criticisms of weaknesses in past programs are valuable if used to improve as well as to expand future programs. Important guidelines for aid can emerge from such discussions. These might include the following list of imperatives.

1. Provide types of aid that will best reduce inequality of opportunity to those countries which will do the most with it. Concentrate on long-run increases in productivity in developing countries rather than programs that fit our own economic needs or political interests. Help nations to help themselves. Give preference to countries that show strong interest in basic reforms toward greater economic equality and serious intent to extend political liberties as quickly as possible.

2. Separate military and economic assistance to avoid a false picture of the amounts provided for economic aid. Place less comparative emphasis on military assistance, which may encourage countries to buy tanks instead of trains and to build barracks instead of schools.

3. Channel a higher percentage of our funds through international agencies. Sound international administration more easily avoids "welfare imperialism," enforces standards with less negative reaction, and allows receiving nations also to return such nonmaterial cultural gifts as they can provide through a common world pool of reciprocal sharing.

4. Instead of shaping other nations in our image, allow freedom for the self-development of peoples. Show deep

appreciation for their cultures and desires. Attach to our grants as few "strings" as possible, thus joining liberation to development. Be alert to unique conditions and possibilities. For example, where there are many mouths to feed and unemployed hands to put to work, recognize the need for rural development, and, at least temporarily, for labor-intensive production.

These last two guidelines suggest a view of development in broader terms than the economic. From this perspective we are all in some respects undeveloped nations needing help from one another. Economically poorer nations do need technological productivity through division of labor, scientific invention, and economically defensible machines. But we, too, need resources which the Third World can help supply, such as a less materialistic definition of life purpose, ecologically sounder processes, a less frantic and more contemplative existence, the greater intimacy and interpersonal caring characteristic of more rural or familial cultures, and freedom from the tyranny of machines and from the small group that controls the machines. Before the developing nations lose these indigenous values to the extent we have, can they develop a better synthesis of values that can become a model for all of us? Can we, as part of the common pool of world resources, provide larger amounts of capital and technical assistance to them at the same time that they send us specialized teachers and advisers to strengthen our own resources in other aspects of culture? Such a network of interdependency and mutual aid could contribute much to international understanding and peace.

WORLD NEED AND NEW LIFE-STYLES

Economic assistance from the United States has not been as generous as we like to think. The picture of the

United States as the world's Santa Claus fades when one looks closely at the statistics. From 2 percent of our gross national product contributed to Marshall Plan aid to Europe, we have dropped to about one quarter of one percent of gross national product for all foreign aid. In commenting on this, Edward Fried suggested that Marshall Plan aid "stemmed from conviction; the current program is the result of habit."[13] Our official contributions for development assistance as a percentage of gross national product in 1975 ranked us 14th among the 17 industrialized members of the Development Assistance Committee of the Organization for Economic Cooperation and Development. Our percentage figure was less than one third the rate for Sweden and the Netherlands, and less than one half the figure for Portugal, France, and Canada.[14] While we have contributed a larger amount of money, the significant figure is the percentage of our total available production that we give. We really cannot delete from the Bible the statement, "Every one to whom much is given, of him will much be required" (Luke 12:48).

One can argue for an increase in our economic assistance grants on grounds of self-interest. Economic aid does stimulate world trade. It allows us to live in a more peaceful world. It helps the U.S. economy by providing more prosperous customers who are better able to buy our products. In a closely interdependent world, nations are roped together like mountain climbers. When one slips, all feel the tug. Depression, inflation, terrorism, and war are no respecters of national boundaries. It is in our national interest that disprivileged areas develop stable governments and economic strength in order to resist infiltration by totalitarian imperialisms. The bacteria of extremism find congenial hosts in empty stomachs and in frustrated minds. In a real sense, development programs abroad are also an investment in our own peace, prosperity, and freedom.

National incentives are always scrambled. When a narrow, selfish nationalism becomes too prominent in our mixture of motives, we poison the aid package by introducing undesirable and self-defeating features. If our primary motive is egoistic, we are likely to be too protective of our own profit and less enthusiastic about making common cause with the poor. Our assurances of genuine friendship and caring are received as less convincing. Our response is likely to be less sacrificial than it ought to be and more delayed than it must be in a time of exploding expectations in the Third and Fourth Worlds. When nations begin to rationalize their privileges, their capacity for self-deception and hypocrisy must never be underestimated.

Neither must the capacity of a nation for more other-regarding conduct be too heavily discounted. Discussing the altruistic grounds for Sweden's high percentage of gross national product devoted to economic assistance, Gunnar Myrdal said, "It is unrealistic and self-defeating to distrust the moral forces in a nation."[15] A 1972 poll of the U.S. public by the Overseas Development Council showed considerable resistance to increases in specific government-aid programs. At the same time, when the question was put in more general terms, 68 percent favored "the United States giving assistance to underdeveloped countries"—a higher percentage than in previous surveys in 1958 and 1966. A major reason for the contrast was found to be that the public was ill informed about government economic assistance programs, the immensity of world poverty, and the comparatively low level of our contributions. Furthermore, the grounds for objection tended to be not so much to assistance programs per se as to the abuses which respondents felt had crept into the programs. The reasons for favoring aid were primarily based on moral and humanitarian grounds.[16] This points to the crucial need to clarify the specific meanings of our generalized goodwill.

Public policy results from a convergence of enlightened self-interest and spontaneous altruistic response to human need. One of the major assignments to the church is to nurture and give specific content to the altruistic orientation of love. We have yet to learn the profound meaning in the words of Jesus, "Whoever would save his life will lose it, and whoever loses his life for my sake will find it" (Matt. 16:25). It makes a decisive difference whether "save his life" or "lose his life for my sake" describes a person's strongest and most basic commitment. Is our most compelling drive toward astute action in order to preserve private interest? Or is it toward an overwhelming and spontaneous concern for God and neighbor that brings gains to the self as a subordinate value or unsought by-product? The policies of governments will be sounder when a larger number of citizens are responsibly searching for realistic ways to express a more basically altruistic motivation.

To improve our national policy, we need a massive uprising of public opinion to convince our government that we are not Caesar with respect to imperial power, and that we are not Dives with respect to our material resources. The transition in attitude and action may be speeded up as threats of nuclear devastation or environmental breakdown become more obvious, and as a greater pressure of militant demands is felt from the poor. Without remarkable acceleration in ethical action, we will share responsibility for the holocaust to come. As President Lyndon B. Johnson said of economic development in Latin America, "Time is not our ally."

The urgency applies not only to national policy but also to individual life-style. We have already pointed out that sufficiently raising living standards among the poor of the world is possible only as we reduce our own material affluence. It is the intention of God that economic resources be used for the fullest possible meeting of the greatest human need. So long as dehumanizing poverty is so widespread in the world, this guideline for stewardship would seem to leave little for a more fortunate individual to spend on personal wants. There is almost always a greater need elsewhere.

We might argue that God also calls us to be faithful in our stewardship of life energy as well as of our material goods. We might then justify spending on ourselves what is essential for effectiveness in a worthwhile vocation. Such a standard of functional simplicity might justify enough calories and vitamins to remain energetic, but it would not allow nutritionally unnecessary desserts. Dependable transportation might be defensible, but not extra chrome trimming or superfluous horsepower for a car. Do we need to add an extra room while others lack a single room? Or build an additional cupboard while there are children without a cup? We do not quickly judge other affluent persons in these matters, for we do not know their full situation. There may be unique needs and circumstances that justify different expenditures. But all of us need honestly to confront the proposition that property does not exist primarily for the pleasure of the owner but for the welfare of humankind. The great religions of the world have taught a life of moderation, compassion, and enlightenment. They have agreed on the evils of rapacity, greed, and materialism.

Our customary contentment with self-indulgence repeats what the cumulative experience of history has shown to be enervating, exploitative, and the prelude to collapse. Nevertheless, success in life among us is still too much seen in terms of physical comforts and gadgets. Television commercials and newspaper advertisements reverse the verdict of the Bible in their attempt to teach us that a person's life *does* "consist in the abundance of his possessions" (compare Luke 12:15). It has been commonly accepted that in a healthy economy the only acceptable direction for wages and profits is up, even when this means waste of resources in comparatively useless luxury. If this aspect of our culture remains dominant, ours may become the kind of infatuation with decadence that precedes the fall of a civilization. In a basic challenge to prevailing immorality, we need to learn that bigger is not necessarily better, that more is not always an improvement. What is a value up to a point frequently becomes an evil beyond that point. An overdose of medicine may become a poison. When material comforts pass the point of vocational effectiveness, we have turned from creativity toward collapse. Those who then still continue to build larger barns deserve the Biblical label "fool" (Luke 12: 20).

There is also happily a more caring side to our national nature. We are also compassionate and creative, seeking justice and loving mercy. We are beginning to recognize that, as Charles Birch told the 1975 assembly of the World Council of Churches, "The rich must live more simply that the poor may simply live." Many are horrified when they learn that in 1973 while government disbursements for foreign economic assistance were about 3 billion dollars, we in the United States were at the same time spending 7.8 billion for toilet articles and preparations, 13.6 billion for tobacco products, and 21.5 billion for alcoholic beverages.[17]

Legislation can reduce some types of waste or inefficiency. Business policy can do something about advertising and production priorities. For the most part, however, reformed standards of consumption are matters for individual and family action. Instead of being enforced as public requirement, they can become part of the witness of the Christian community, hoping to persuade others to help change the social climate. Growing numbers are now reducing personal expenditures and increasing their contributions to social need. For such persons, the decision to buy what one wants does not depend on "Can I afford this?" but "Is this the loving thing to do for all the persons on earth now and in future generations?" Every conscientious individual and family needs seriously to consider reducing or eliminating a lengthy list of common expenditures. Instead of winning status by conspicuous material consumption, Christians ought to be conspicuous for their nonconsumption. Should we not now take pride in repairing and conserving instead of replacing and discarding? Can we now justify buying big cars, color television sets, electric can openers, dishwashers, steaks frequently, private swimming pools, or all the gadgets we have? Where should we draw the line if we remember children in dismal want and irreplaceable resources in diminishing supply?

A reduced *material* standard of living can be combined with a rise in the *total* standard of living. Functional simplicity of life does not need to mean economic depression or stagnation. We would be paying fewer persons to manufacture cosmetics or supersonic planes, but we would still be manufacturing essential materials for those who need them here and in other parts of the world. Concerning proposals for a "no growth" economy, poor nations have sometimes suspected that rich countries, having climbed to a comfortable level themselves, now want to kick the ladder down behind them. We must give no grounds for such a suspicion. In addition to manufacturing for others, we could keep the economy moving without a recession because, while employing fewer people in manufacturing luxury goods, we would be hiring more persons to provide services through musical groups, adult education, meditation retreats, national parks, personal-growth groups, social reform movements, and research centers in the relationship of religion and health. Instead of a no growth economy, this would be a "new growth" or "selective growth" economy. At the same time, the "knowledge intensive" and "feeling intensive" activities involved would be less resource-depleting and pollution-producing, thus leaving more of the earth's physical wealth for raising material standards of the poor and meeting the essential needs of future generations.

People who are poor in soul are likely to try to multiply material possessions in a vain effort to satisfy their inner hungers. By shifting our preoccupations to a greater extent from physical and material things to social and spiritual values, more human hungers can be satisfied. We may possess fewer gadgets, but more continuous enjoyment and complete fulfillment. By removing existing blinders and barriers, we can discover beauty and friends and literature and prayer and important social causes. With these emphases, we become far richer than with the kind of luxury we now regard as the peak of achievement. We may then learn more of what was meant by "having nothing, and yet possessing everything" (II Cor. 6:10).

In ways we have previously discussed, our scrambled priorities and our perpetuation of injustice are related to the continued threat of modern war. As the saintly Quaker John Woolman once wrote, "May we look upon our treasures, the furniture of our houses, and our garments, and try whether the seeds of war have nourishment in these our possessions." The roots of war are to be found not only in the way nations handle political power but also in the manner peoples use economic resources. One of the places that peace begins is in my personal checkbook—as well as in my ballots and letters to legislators on economic assistance programs.

10

A New International Economic Order

"THE WORLD APPEARS to be on the verge of one of the great economic, social, and political discontinuities of history." In these words, Theodore Hesburgh summarized one of the major conclusions of much recent research.[1] The intricate involvement of all nations in a new network of economic relationships brings consequences that cannot be handled by traditional structures. Society as it is now organized cannot be sustained indefinitely. New ecological realities and the modern technology of weaponry demand change. If plagues such as hunger are to be cured, we must go beyond humanitarian relief and agricultural improvement to basic structural change. Beyond even such compelling matters, exciting new possibilities now exist for creative world relationships and unprecedented human development. Actualizing promises of such magnitude also requires important changes in social patterns as well as in spiritual understanding of the goals of life.

The necessary changes in structure are not as comprehensive as some would have us believe. A great deal of the old will still remain. Our ancestors did well in moving us thus far along the way. Yet, as in any dynamic, progressive situation, changed conditions and new possibilities require significant alterations. These must become the contribution of the present generation if humankind is to preserve viable civilization or even continued life. In general, the required changes move farther from narrow national interests to global concerns, from competitive selfishness to cooperative goodwill, and from domination and exploitation by the powerful to universal participation in joint planning for the common good. In short, we must move toward international economic practices that are more consistent with the ethical wisdom of our religious tradition.

INTERNATIONAL MEANINGS FOR ECONOMIC JUSTICE

Justice in the sense of "to each his due" has been interpreted in many contradictory ways to defend the privileges of various groups and classes. When justice is thought of as the closest approximation to the norm of love which is possible within the ambiguities of large group relationships, it should have a powerfully transforming effect on our conceptions of proper distribution. That which is due each person then becomes the most complete satisfaction of needs and liberation of potentialities that the resources of the earth make possible. Present arrangements fall short of this not only because vast inequalities of opportunity exist but also because serious barriers block rich and poor alike. The rich have limitations placed on their moral and spiritual growth, and the poor on their physical and material development. As Kurt Waldheim, Secretary-General of the United Nations, wrote: "The international system of economic and trade relations which was devised 30 years ago is now manifestly inadequate for the needs of the world community as a whole. The charge against that order in the past was that it worked well for the affluent and against the poor. It cannot now even be said that it works well for the affluent."[2]

Present arrangements favor the rich nations in many of their immediate results, though in long-run economic and spiritual consequences they handicap rich and poor alike. Countries with disparate economic strength do not bargain as equals. World monetary and trade policies especially benefit the industrialized nations. The natural resources of poorer nations have been exploited, and their economies shaped to meet the needs of the rich nations. Raw materials and primary products, which are the chief exports of the developing world, are subject to serious price fluctuations. At the same time, the manufacturing industries of the developing world are restricted in growth because they cannot export through the tariff walls of the developed world. All these factors make it easier for the rich to grow richer. They also make it harder to close the gap between rich and poor.

Developing nations are asking for higher and more stable prices for commodities they are able to export, such as copper, bauxite, or coffee. A drop in the price of coffee, for example, can completely erase the effects of our assistance funds to coffee-producing countries. If such a price drop coincides with an inflationary price rise for manufactured goods which the developing nation must import, the effect is devastating. More stable prices for the primary products which the developing nations sell might be gained by devices such as international stockpiles, or by compensatory financing arrangements. Without such innovations, more developing countries will try to form the kind of joint marketing association that has so markedly raised the price of oil. If we neglect their interests, we have no right to expect that they will regard ours.

Developing nations could also earn higher incomes if they processed some of their primary commodities inside their own country and exported the finished products. There is often more capital for development to be earned by selling shirts instead of cotton, or steel instead of iron ore. Developing countries ask for such tariff adjustments as will allow them to develop those industries in which they may have comparatively favorable conditions for production. Infant industries require temporary protection until they are sufficiently established to test fairly their competitive advantage. Economists point out that production in the areas of greatest comparative advantage is a kind of international division of labor which benefits consumers everywhere with lower prices. For this reason, tariff arrangements temporarily favorable to the developing nations are in the long run likely to be favorable also to the richer nations.

Developing countries are also handicapped when international economic decision-making is so largely in the hands of those who are already wealthy and powerful. For example, international lending agencies tend to be dominated by the great powers. There seems to be little hope of immediate change unless the attitude of unilateral charity gives way to the acceptance of mutual justice. Charity from the rich is always infected with paternalism. The giver restricts the freedom of the recipient, at least to the extent of deciding how much is to be given and for what general purpose. A more democratic process is not likely to be voluntarily adopted unless the developed nations recognize that what seemed more profitable for them in the past is no longer in their long-run best interest. Their clinging to present policies can only mean reaping a bitter harvest in the future. This note of realism is reinforced by compassionate empathy for the powerless. The New Testament points us toward a relationship in which the parts of the whole do not subordinate each other, but rather "if one member suffers, all suffer together; if one member is honored, all rejoice together" (I Cor. 12:26). Some aspects of present competitiveness encourage us to do just the opposite, to rejoice at another nation's failure, to be disappointed at another's success. We need to recognize that the successful have no right to block the success of others. Every person has the right to participate in the making of those policy decisions by which his or her welfare is affected.

Poor nations can be expected increasingly to rebel against having their destinies determined by others. Whether there is enough statesmanship and morality in the rich nations to share their decision-making power will largely determine the nature of world politics in the coming generation. In reply to the demands of the Third World, Secretary of State Henry Kissinger at the 1975 Seventh Special Session of the UN Assembly announced: "We have heard your voices. We embrace your hopes. We will join your efforts." It remains to be seen whether this was rhetoric designed to buy time for further foot-dragging, or whether this indeed foreshadowed genuine and prompt changes in U.S. policy.

PROMISE AND PERIL IN MULTINATIONAL CORPORATIONS

Increasingly important in shaping the future of the world are huge multinational corporations, each under a unified management doing business in many countries of the world. In 1970 multinationals reportedly accounted for one sixth of the world's output, including 40 percent of the world's industrial production.[3] The goods and services produced by the biggest three hundred multinational corporations are estimated as greater than the gross national product of every country in the world except the United States.[4] If present trends continue, it is estimated that by the end of the next decade a few hundred corporations will control 50 percent to 80 percent of the essential factors of production in the noncommunist world.[5]

A transnational organization of economic enterprise can theoretically provide advantages to benefit the entire world population. Barnet and Müller point out, "The men who run the global corporations are the first in history with the organization, technology, money, and ideology to make a credible try at managing the world as an integrated unit."[6] It is possible for a huge corporation to tap financial support, physical resources, and human skill from around the globe and to combine these factors in more efficient processes. Knowledge, technology, and skill could be shared from country to country. Capital, employment opportunities, and consumer goods could be brought to the poorer nations. In numerous fields in which large-scale enterprise is an advantage, substantial savings could be reaped through mass production, planned distribution, expanded research, and coordinated decisions. These savings could be shared in lower prices to consumers and higher wages to workers. This is the dream of many of the managers of the global corporations. Yet, in actual practice some of the inherent characteristics of multinational corporations limit or block the realization of the dream.

In a day of global interdependence, the problem is not international enterprise. International cooperation is increasingly a necessity. The problem raised by multinational corporations is centralized control of vital resources by comparatively small groups for private profit.

As one example, one of the important contributions multinationals could theoretically make is to supply private capital from outside sources to developing countries. But the desire to maximize profit and minimize risks sharply reduces the amount of additional capital that is actually made available. Much of the capital used by multinationals is derived from profits made within the developing country, or in borrowing from its banks (which leaves less to be borrowed by local enterprises). A large outside corporation may use local capital for gaining control of more enterprises. By repatriating profits based on these locally generated funds it can actually contribute to the decapitalization of developing countries.

When business units approach the size of the multinationals, or cosmocorps, they tend to have the powers of a monopoly. In a situation of oligopoly, with only a few giants in a field, economists find reasons for saying that monopoly conditions essentially prevail. The area of oligopoly control continues to expand. A successful multinational corporation can use profits from one country to drive out competition in other countries. Or profits from one product, like oil, can be used to extend control into other fields, like coal or natural gas. A bigger company can often outadvertise smaller companies and thereby corner a larger share of the market. Locally owned small business is at a decided disadvantage. A meaningful free-enterprise system tends to disappear.

Oligopolistic corporations can administer prices, fixing them at the point of greatest profit for themselves. In effect, this becomes the power to levy a tax on the consumers of the world. Where it seems in the interest of the company to conceal the actual rate of profit, devices like transfer pricing can be used. A parent company can sell products or raw materials to a subsidiary in another country at highly inflated prices. By charging comparatively little above these inflated "costs" the subsidiary company can conceal from the host country the actual corporate profits involved.

By advertising, influence over the mass media, and the selection of goods to be produced, global corporations can increasingly standardize for the entire world what people will eat, drink, and wear. For example, an invasion of movies and television shows from the United States is shaping Latin-American culture in a foreign image. This threatens the important values to be found in cultural pluralism. It also may be exporting the worst rather than the best features of an industrial culture. In all these respects, consumers are paying the costs of their own exploitation.

This imperialistic drive to maximize profits tends also to speed up environmental collapse and the exhaustion of natural resources. Especially is this true when the biggest profits are to be made by using in other countries the technology, production plans, and advertising campaigns already developed for the home country. This may result in a saving of cost, but to a significant extent it also encourages the rest of the world to adopt the unnecessary luxury and the materialistic lifestyle of the richest nations. Such a "global shopping center," designed only for affluent enclaves, both delays the production of necessities and more rapidly uses up the minerals, soil, and clean air of the earth.

It is true that global corporations create numerous jobs. Their corporate practices may also create and prolong an even more widespread unemployment in the population as a whole. Importing a technology already designed for a developed country may not fit the conditions of a developing nation. Where there are large numbers of unemployed, a capital-intensive and labor-saving technology is often less appropriate, at least in the short run, than a labor-intensive mode of production or than the "intermediate technology" of which Ernest Schumacher speaks.[7] Mounting unemployment plus private control of the profits produced by the machines also contribute to a more unequal concentration of income. Even while gross national product may be increased, it is at the cost of human misery. As Brazilian president Emílio Médici once described it, "The economy is doing very well, but the people are not."[8]

Even if by some magic wand multinational corporations could be made much more altruistic and perfectly efficient in serving human needs, they would still be denying full liberty to by far the most persons on earth. A small group, often outside one's own country, would be making life-changing decisions for the general citizenry. The people deserve a greater voice in their own destiny. Both by its sheer size and by its ability to maneuver autonomously beyond the control of both host and headquarters countries, a multinational corporation can become not only a business enterprise but also a semisovereign political power. The ability of multinationals to move production and capital from country to country weakens the ability of even developed nations to keep their own economy healthy through tax, labor, or monetary legislation. Even the people of the United States are less likely to achieve their planning goals when global corporations are planning toward different objectives. By dummy corporations abroad and intracompany transfers, corporations can make it appear that profits were made in low-tax countries. Thus, in high-tax countries they avoid the taxes they should be paying and shift the tax burden to the rest of the taxpayers. When corporations shift production to low-wage areas, our present attempts to establish minimum wages and full employment tend to be frustrated. By the threat of shifting production abroad, labor's bargaining power is decreased and a trend toward inequality in this country is intensified.

Multinationals are one of the most powerful forces shaping the destinies of both developing and developed nations. They are also one of the most difficult concentrations of power to make democratically accountable. They have demonstrated their capacity to influence elections and to unseat unfriendly governments. Is there any way of securing the benefits of the multinationals without their ill effects? Can we gain the economies of large-scale production wherever they apply, and still control the goals of the enterprise? Is international economic solidarity possible without at the same time increasing tensions between exploited and exploiters? There are four general possibilities for improvement.

1. Increasingly responsible policies might develop because of the growing ethical sensitivity of stockholders and management. In some respects morality is reinforced by sound business acumen. For example, growing resentment in developing nations is likely to threaten the position of existing multinationals. Their very capacity to survive requires building "more symmetric organizations that permit full participation by interests in the less developed nations and are responsive to their needs."[9] Both the drive of long-term self-interest and humanitarian motives may lead to further self-restraint embodied in a more widely accepted code of conduct for transnational corporations. This might include a developing trend toward more joint-venture enterprises, or even fade-out by transfer of ownership to citizens or governments of the host country. It is encouraging to note the number of business leaders who do recognize the need for humanitarian reforms. Yet this approach alone is scarcely likely to be sufficient. Enlightened business leaders are often limited by the unscrupulous competition of others.

2. Another possibility is regulation of the more socially detrimental practices by both host and headquarters countries. For example, legislation might forbid undue interference in the political affairs of a country, or capital drain by excessive repatriation of profits. While this is essential, it is also difficult. Regulation by host countries is hampered so long as the United States

continues unjustified intervention on behalf of U.S.-based corporations. For both host and headquarters countries the expense of the investigative procedures necessary to detect violation in a vast corporation is forbidding. An activity proscribed in one country can sometimes be shifted to another. Because of the power of a cosmocorp, the regulated easily become the regulators.

3. Effective controls increasingly will require international authority in agencies like the United Nations. With respect to many of their operations between nations, multinationals now exist in something like a legal vacuum. With no laws, or differing laws from country to country, the corporations by various devices can choose their own regulation. As an immediate remedial step, fact-finding and publicity by international agencies could have significant influence. Effective control, however, requires a body of international law to apply to such intricate and huge international business operations. A similar need exists in postal delivery, airplane hijacking, and pollution of international waterways. This requires a revitalization and reorganization of international political institutions to keep pace with recent revolutionary changes in the world economy.

4. If regulation fails, there may be no alternative to nationalization or socialization of some holdings of international enterprise within particular countries. The right of nationalization by a country of its basic resources must be recognized. So must the obligation to pay a fair compensation, the determination of which may take into account any exorbitant profits already taken out of a country. In some cases, as in mining of the seabed, internationalization may be more appropriate than nationalization.

INTERNATIONAL NETWORKS OF ECONOMIC INTERDEPENDENCE

From their elaborate computerized analysis of various possible ways of dealing with the current oil crisis and the food crisis, Mihajlo Mesarovič and Eduard Pestel conclude that global cooperation offers much better outcomes for all concerned than do various forms of conflict. They are convinced by the evidence "that the emergence of a new world system is a matter of necessity, not preference, and that that system must be built on cooperation." They further emphasize an inevitable concomitant conclusion which may not be easily accepted by nations and peoples. "Cooperation by definition connotes interdependence. Increasing interdependence between nations and regions must then translate as a decrease in independence."[10] We cannot work through our shortages of fuel and food without nations' giving up some of their independence.

This is not to suggest lack of freedom for autonomous action. Most economic enterprises can continue to operate within whatever framework of regulation or ownership that individual states may consider desirable. A dull, static uniformity is not a defensible goal. A wide range of cultural and economic pluralism is both possible and valuable. Varieties of capitalistic, socialistic, or mixed systems can continue to exist in different countries. At the same time, at several crucial points, international organization is as necessary for economic affairs as it is for selected political matters. Already nations have accepted international action when the need was quite obvious. Through the specialized agencies of the United Nations, common procedures are accepted for such matters as delivering mail, controlling air traffic, or allocating radio frequencies. Emerging realities now lengthen the list of activities in which we must obviously hang together or we will all hang separately. Urgent necessity may stimulate widespread adherence to treaties recommended by international agencies. For example, the International Maritime Consultative Organization has worked out a convention for preventing pollution of the sea by oil. The International Atomic Energy Agency has established standards for the disposal of nuclear wastes. The full effect has not yet been seen of UN-sponsored conferences on the law of the seas, population, environment, and human settlements. It is in the overriding interests of each country that there should be some implementation of coordinated policy in regard to weather modification, pollution of air and sea, economic depression and inflation, international crime, mining of ocean resources, and certain activities of multinational corporations. Unmanageable apart from international action are genocidal and terracidal threats like nuclear weaponry, environmental collapse, the consequences of inordinate economic inequality, population growth, and resource depletion.

Humankind has not yet found an organized system for sufficiently reconciling the driving ambitions of nation-states with the deeper unities of world society. But unless we are quite suicidal, this deepening crisis is likely to demonstrate the utter necessity of new forms of supranational authority. There is an inexorable, exponential progression involved in some of our major threats. Some progressions, like those related to population or some forms of economic growth and pollution, double in a given period of time. The rate of increase becomes a constant acceleration which finally becomes uncontrollable. If a tiny noxious plant in a pond doubles in size every day, it encroaches very slowly at first. It may trigger no remedial action until the pond is one quarter filled. By then it is too late to launch a lengthy cleanup program, for in two more days the plant will crowd out everything else in the pond. Existing circumstances require intelligent foresight and prompt anticipatory action through international agencies. An aroused electorate in the United States must demand a dramatic change in our comparatively listless and languid support of the United Nations. International action must quickly be given a higher priority on our national agenda.

It is now a requirement of both justice and survival that in the United Nations and in international negotiation, the United States actively support the legitimate aspirations of the Third World. Our problems with the "automatic majority" built around smaller developing nations in the United Nations would become much less troublesome if we recognized our common interests with those nations and established ourselves as an understanding ally. We could then more often add the attractiveness of moral leadership to the coercive threat of our economic and military power. Robert Heilbroner has reminded us that in the Third World "the central, inescapable, and indispensable precondition for 'economic' development is political and social change on a wrenching and tearing scale."[11] The United States has characteristically opposed necessary revolutionary action, in the sense of fundamental, rapid change. The result is that new regimes aiding the common people are likely to be bitterly anti-American. In the minds of the great majority of the world's population, we dare not allow ourselves to be identified with unjust old systems, while Communist nations, with all their faults, are thought of as supporting improved new arrangements.

We can establish greater credibility for our international good intentions if we embody in our own domestic structures less of discrimination and domination and more of justice, liberty, and equal opportunity. It is of no use to tell developing nations to change their culture (for example, to report to work on time) if we do not change ours (to a lower material standard of living). It is hypocritical to urge other countries to change their social structures (as by land reform) if we do not do the same (as by reducing inequalities of wealth and political influence). As Alan Geyer put it, "The advent of effective and humane institutions of world governance depends, in considerable measure, upon the achievement of effective and humane governance within the world's wealthiest and most powerful nation."[12]

In the long run any world leadership we contribute will depend upon the model we develop within our own country and on our ability and willingness to help meet the broad needs of other nations. If we intend to maintain our position as a "great power" only through our natural resources and technical skill, we are doomed to lose whatever leadership we have. Our skills will increasingly be matched by educational achievements in many more lands. Our natural resources will finally run out while some other nations still retain more critical materials than we will have. We will then go the way of all world leaders of the past and at best remain a second- or third-rate power. To resent those who point out this plain fact of history is as futile as breaking the thermometer to cure a fever. It is only in shared leadership of an improved and enlarged kind that the United States can fulfill the promise of its best heritage.

We need a new cultural definition of what it means to be a "great power." Nations are called to a new life-style more ethically defensible within the realities of the modern world. Our current description of a strong nation is still largely in terms of the ability to dominate and exploit other nations through military might or economic power. Speaking of powerful monarchs who flaunt great castles, Jeremiah asked, "Do you think you are a king because you compete in cedar?" (Jer. 22:15). The time has come to apply to nations the criterion of Jesus, "He who is greatest among you shall be your servant" (Matt. 23:11). In a closely interdependent world, national prestige must come to be associated not with power over other nations but with creative participation in decision-making with others. In a time of inordinate economic inequality, greatness for the rich nations is to be marked not so much by further acquisition as by divestiture of unjust advantages.

This will increasingly give to all nations equal access to basic materials. In view of scarcities in irreplaceable resources, both developing and developed countries may see the desirability of a *material* standard of living lower than the developed nations now have and higher than the developing nations possess. The *total* standard of living can be much higher by increasing the availability and enjoyment of nonmaterial social, intellectual, aesthetic, moral, and religious values. When necessary physical essentials are more nearly assured, humankind may then direct more creative energy toward such a new order of values. If we successfully move through this transition, the vocational preoccupation of future generations can be less with goods and gadgets, and more with personal services. We can spend more time helping each other deepen interpersonal relationships, work for social change, appreciate or produce music and art, share philosophical insights, or develop methods for meditation and mystical experience.

Over such values we do not need to fight. They are available in abundance. They are multiplied by sharing. Material values must be defended and hoarded to be retained. Were a ton of copper to be divided, each of two parties would have only half a ton. On the other hand, when an idea, a character trait, a meaningful relationship, an aesthetic appreciation, or a religious experience is shared, both parties can simultaneously possess it in its entirety. All nations can then be number one without having to push other nations into a number two spot. International trade or exchange in social and spiritual values has fewer destructively competitive features.

Peace will also become less precarious insofar as we consciously expand worldwide networks of international interdependence. As we increase global division of labor and trade, engage in joint medical and social research, or belong to more international scholarly or cultural associations, each country will find itself a member of a number of groups, some sharing a worldwide membership. Antagonisms in one group relationship may be reduced because of the benefits of cooperation in other relationships. If appropriate present trends can be accelerated, we will all find ourselves vitally dependent on a complex network of relationships for essentials such as sufficient food and clean air, physical health and psychological fulfillment, national security and human existence. We will not be able to afford to break the intricate ties of international relationships which will have become the delivery systems for those values we all want most. Nations will have more vested interests in avoiding hostile relationships. Tensions will continue, yet the more good we get out of peaceful cooperation the less likely we are to attempt to disrupt it. Accommodation will then be encouraged because the rewards of peaceful living will have become greater, rather than because the horrors of deterrence and war will have bécome worse. As intense economic competition has preceded many past wars, so vital economic and social interdependence may precede future détente. National interests in security and well-being will more obviously be best served by maintaining peace.

Whether or not we carry international interdependence still further, a considerable amount of it is already a fact of life. National states acting alone can no longer perform the functions that both theologians and political scientists list as their reasons for being. Neither freedom nor security can be nationally provided when another powerful nation launches a military attack or touches off a worldwide economic depression. The prosperity of producers in one land depends on the prosperity of consumers in other lands. Isolated states cannot provide full justice for their citizens so long as other nations act as sole judges of their own cases. The jurisdiction of a single country is no longer wide enough to protect its citizens against new perils of exploitation, terrorism, hijacking, or invasion originating in other countries. Those who face contemporary realities must know that universally desired superordinate goals, like peace, prosperity, and freedom, cannot now be achieved by any nation or group of nations alone, but only by all nations together. Governments must act in more harmonious concert if they are to continue to exist at all.

Yet the unification of humankind in God's creation and universal concern is still denied by our autonomous and divisive social structures. An obligation to inclusive relationship and service is an inescapable consequence of our religious commitment. Because we are concerned about the welfare of each individual person, we are now forced to organize global society. Cooperation must be given an organized structure on a world scale.

This still requires a considerable conversion of popular attitudes toward both international structures and ethical priorities. To accomplish the necessary changes, Mihajlo Mesarovič and Eduard Pestel point out that we need both a "horizontal" restructuring of the systems of relationships among nations and also a shift in the "vertical" structure of the value systems and goals of persons.[13] Can we now see our country as only one region while the world has become our nation? Can we feel the hurt and the want of millions in the developing world as though they were members of our larger family? Can we know that material goods are to be conserved also for future generations and that a simpler life may liberate us to higher social and spiritual values? For our own survival and fulfillment we earthlings require a new loyalty, beyond clan, tribe, and nation, as Barbara Ward and René Dubos phrased it, to "our single, beautiful, and vulnerable planet Earth."[14] To this we are led by an even more ultimate loyalty to God, who is the loving sovereign of the universe.

11

Resources of Churches
and Resistances to Change

THE ONLY ROAD to a more durable peace has two parallel lanes. They lead politically from unlimited national sovereignty to limited world organization, and economically from profit-motivated, nationalistic competition to cooperation for the common good over a wider range of values. Are such major movements possible?

Considering the magnitude of the changes involved and the entrenched power of the traditionally privileged, the prospect would seem to be hopeless. The prospect becomes even more dismal when we add the strong contemporary mood of helplessness and apathy among citizens who in a democracy are supposedly the determinative force in national policy. Ward and Dubos have suggested that the picture now seems to many so gloomy and irreversible that "the average citizen's response is to go out and buy a can of beer. If nothing can be done to escape the onward rush of some irresistible eco-doom, then why take the trouble even to return the can?"[1]

Indeed we cannot expect the cessation of controversy and conflict in human affairs. Given the nature of persons and the necessity of disagreement with any establishment if there is to be significant improvement, conflict is to be expected or even welcomed. But conflict does not need to become war. The military response is not biologically determined. Mass killing techniques to

213

advance group purposes were social inventions. They can be replaced with other innovations. We have made similar changes in the past. We still have economic competition and even exploitation, but we no longer have an established system of slavery. We continue to have irresponsible defamation on the political hustings, but we do not commonly impress subordinates into private feudal armies or assassinate opponents. With all the discouraging difficulties we face, there are also at least four grounds for hope in international affairs.

1. On the major components necessary to a more adequate foreign policy, American public opinion appears to be near the tilt point. That is, the population is so evenly divided that it is not at all hopeless to build a majority coalition. Especially is this true since it is always an articulate, attentive, or informed minority that gives leadership to the opinion of the general public. It is this politically active minority which has the greatest influence on public decision, at the same time as the total prevailing public mood sets limits to what leaders can do.

The traditional consensus about unilateral, interventionist foreign policy has been badly cracked by the Vietnam war, and by the growing consciousness of new ecological and weapons threats. While opinion has not yet gone far enough, it has already moved a long way in desirable directions. Polls have shown strong support for our membership in the United Nations and for some kind of aid to the poor of the world. This provides a foundation for education in more specific contemporary meanings of these basic predispositions. Should there be a notable turn of world events or an emergence of charismatic political leadership or of a more active peace movement, the chances for improvement in public policy are about as good as the chances for continuation of our present disastrous course. It is not at all inconceivable that in the near future politicians in general cannot hope to be elected unless they give stronger support to international organization, world development, and global justice.

2. The spur of crisis is likely to speed up the pace of social change. It is true that a threat too great and unrelieved may increase hopelessness, apathy, and traditional biases. But when there is also a powerful presentation of a way out of the threatening situation, serious crises in the past have often become catalysts for constructive change. A cluster of related crises are now becoming more dramatically obvious. There are also possible solutions, embodied in ideas whose time has come, if they are persuasively presented. It has often been stressed that utopian ideas are useless and even dangerous. They waste energy in proposals so far ahead as to have no chance for adoption. It is equally dangerous to continue to advocate old ideas that lag behind changes already made in the social climate.

3. Motivation for change may well be intensified, since on current issues there is considerable overlap between enlightened self-interest and altruistic concern. Enlightenment added to self-interest takes into account the long run and the total range of consequences. It would lead us to see the domestic benefits of foreign aid, for example, including its spiritual as well as material values, now and to succeeding generations. On this particular issue self-interest could lead to almost the same conclusion as loving concern for suffering people everywhere.

This convergence between self and social interest is not complete, however. What is best for the United States is not necessarily best for the world, even if "best" is given the most comprehensive meaning. In situations of scarcity so great that the long-term interests of all cannot be equally served, a choice between self and others must be made. When four explorers are far from their base camp with only enough provisions to get two back, an ethic of mutuality breaks down. The world today is approaching vital scarcities. By acting soon enough we may still be able largely to avoid that cruel choice. We are more likely to act substantially enough and quickly enough since a surprisingly large number of citizens have shown latent capacities for empathetic goodwill.

Whether or not these capacities are fully awakened, those citizens primarily motivated by long-term self-interest and those motivated by radical love may become allies in advocating a common foreign policy to move us toward our goal. The differing motives can now combine to make it more likely that progressive changes will be adopted. International organization and development can now contribute both to social solidarity and human need and also to our own preservation and fulfillment.

4. There are vast unused resources in both individuals and society which we have never directed toward more peaceful international relations. Within every person lie amazing, dormant potentialities for creative action waiting to be released. Our society embodies a historical accumulation of wholesome interests and predispositions which are ordinarily appealed to in only superficial ways. Our commitments to justice and good will are more often directed toward domestic issues than to foreign policy—and even there the typical appeal has lacked philosophical and moral depth.

There has always been a great struggle in the soul of America that has at various times produced magnanimous as well as nationalistic action, innovative as well as reactionary impulses. In times of grave crisis there has often been an acceleration of innovative response, as recently during the Great Depression of the '30s or in the civil rights struggle. In spite of present public disillusionment and even cynicism about our political institutions, in some respects our democratic processes appear healthier now than for some time past. Our political structures weathered Vietnam and Watergate and more recent revelations of civil crime. Our institutions have also emerged with modest gains in a more alert and demanding electorate, in more active and courageous officials, and in added safeguards for more democratic and effective procedures.

Beyond as well as through all these resources God is active in the world, with a gift of power to those who open their lives to receive it. Seemingly impossible things have been accomplished by those who discovered larger meanings in life and enthusiastically devoted their total capacities to a great cause. The resources which are released through vital relationship with God also remain largely unused in the common round of our lives. Still, God continues to be more eager to give than we are to receive.

None of these observations is strong enough to guarantee a hopeful future. Unless we find ways more fully to utilize these resources we will continue the mediocrity and lethargy that ensure international disaster. None of our more promising possibilities is likely to be fully actualized without a vital and active church. Organized religion could bring unique contributions to match the peculiar needs of fateful times. The church is the one social institution with the specialized function of relating the highest ethical insight to the broadest practical reality. The holistic viewpoint of religion, including both the immediate and the ultimate, can contribute to sounder insights. Religious faith, by deepening motivation and cultivating spiritual power, should produce more effective action.

George W. Ball, Undersecretary of State in the

Kennedy and Johnson Administrations, describes "the central deficiency" in our current foreign policy. "It is not merely too narrow in its focus but too niggardly in its objectives. . . . What is missing . . . is a moral theme to give coherence to what we, as a nation, are trying to do."[2] This is precisely the gift offered by the authentic church.

A basic requirement for making peace possible is a reorientation of public opinion in the United States. As Richard Barnet concludes, "Most people feel incompetent and irrelevant when it comes to foreign affairs."[3] The church with its unique resources and its access in weekly meetings to such a high percentage of the total population has an incomparable opportunity to affect the necessary awakening of competence and the required shift in the direction of public opinion.

Yet the church in international affairs has left most of its resources unused. Overhead groups, like the National and World Councils of Churches, have occasionally organized strong initiatives. Examples are U.S. membership in the United Nations, support for economic assistance, normalizing relationships with the People's Republic of China, or opposing continued intervention in Vietnam. Yet such emphases have been sporadic and weak. The church's betrayal of human need is even worse on the local level, where the most effective dialogue with the citizenry might take place. Ministers seldom preach sermons devoted to international affairs. Congregations typically do not organize serious classes on the subject.[4] Such social action projects as there are more often aim at social welfare and individual relief rather than at basic reform of major social systems. Christian ethics and international affairs demand higher priorities in church programs, budgets, and staff time. The issues involved are complex and crucial enough to deserve higher proportions of all three of these congregational resources.

The church has an inherent source of powerful regeneration which has from time to time caused amazing transformations. Vatican II was such a time of reformation. In several respects it moved the Roman Catholic Church not only abreast but ahead of the movement of history. Much of the Church in Latin America is now giving remarkable leadership in controversial demands for economic justice. In country after country the Church is now the greatest defender of human rights and political freedoms. The steady and growing acceptance, in both liberal and evangelical churches, of the importance of an active social witness may yet prove to be an equally powerful moving of the spirit of God in our land. Such an outcome, however, depends on a much more affirmative response to the leading of God in local congregations, including a more informed analysis of the major needs of contemporary constituencies.

Especially needed is public competence in the fundamental social theory which must be understood before the electorate will consistently support specific measures that become desirable from year to year. The general public does not require the advanced expertise of the specialist. As was pointed out in Chapter 3, citizens do need to evaluate the presuppositions of specialists. For democracy to remain viable, voters need a sufficient, popularized understanding to express intelligent preferences for general directions in policy. This is the role of the electorate in our political process, while more detailed decisions are left to specialized officials held responsible for the outcomes of those decisions. The indispensable basic orientation of citizens now includes an understanding of the nature of modern national security, the necessity and shape of international organization, and goals and directions for international development.

Churches have confined themselves almost completely to generalizations like peace and justice and equal opportunity. Research in the behavioral sciences indicates that the attitudes of hearers are not changed by such generalizations apart from a more concrete analysis. After all, Communists and capitalists, interventionists and isolationists have all convinced themselves that their policies will best achieve those glowingly attractive and delightfully general goals. Affirmation of general goals simply confirms all these contradictory groups in their existing convictions. A more critical analysis of concrete, present situations is needed if opinions are to change.

On the other hand, to deal only with immediate, narrowly specific questions is also inadequate. Pragmatism on day-to-day decisions is dangerous if it is not informed by a policy based on more inclusive considerations. We are more likely, and more promptly, to make more desirable decisions on immediate matters if we have thought through our guidelines for general policy. Without such a frame of reference the public is easily swayed by the mass media or by special interest groups. The intermediate range of education on general policy is now especially necessary. It has been much neglected by the church. Concern for peace needs to be implemented by guidelines more concrete than vast generalizations and more comprehensive than the specific problems that emerge from year to year.

In this middle area of empirically supported guidelines, decisive breaks with the past are now called for. This generation needs to recognize that for certain functions the sovereign nation-state is now obsolete. We need to know that the desire to be the number one nation in the traditional economic sense has become "a meaningless and obscene goal in a world on the brink of famine."[5] We need to feel deeply that our reliance on more destructive military weaponry must quickly be replaced by a more complex, effective, and morally defensible approach to security. These are the chief contributions of responsible specialists in international relations and the major foreign policy emphases required in church programs today. Members of the church must now demand such a contribution from the church. This becomes one of the most basic ways of strengthening the possibility of world peace.

NOTES

Chapter 1
THEOLOGICAL AND ETHICAL PRESUPPOSITIONS

1. Reinhold Niebuhr, *Moral Man and Immoral Society* (Charles Scribner's Sons, 1932), p. 91.
2. *Ibid.*, p. 95.
3. George F. Kennan, *Russia and the West Under Lenin and Stalin* (Little, Brown & Company, Inc., 1960), p. 5.
4. John Adams, quoted in Conrad Cherry, ed., *God's New Israel* (Prentice-Hall, Inc., 1971), p. 65.
5. Article by John Osborn in *The New Republic,* April 10, 1976.
6. Reinhold Niebuhr, *Christian Realism and Political Problems* (Charles Scribner's Sons, 1953), p. 28.
7. Herbert Butterfield, *Christianity and History* (Charles Scribner's Sons, 1950), p. 41.
8. Arthur Schlesinger, Jr., "The Necessary Amorality of Foreign Affairs," *Harper's Magazine,* August 1971.
9. Hans Morgenthau, *In Defense of the National Interest* (Alfred A. Knopf, Inc., 1951), p. 37.
10. George F. Kennan, *Realities of American Foreign Policy* (Princeton University Press, 1954), p. 47.
11. George F. Kennan, "Foreign Policy and Christian Conscience," *The Atlantic Monthly,* May 1959.
12. It is worthwhile to consider how this discussion of assassination is related to the plot to assassinate Hitler in which much-admired Germans were involved, including Dietrich Bonhoeffer. One difference is that the German plot was a revolutionary act by Germans themselves and was not an episode in the conduct of international relations. In the latter context there would be no way of containing the spreading mistrust

that would be created by assassination plots by governments in their relations with other governments.

13. Hans Morgenthau, *Politics Among Nations,* 5th ed. (Alfred A. Knopf, Inc., 1974), pp. 237–241.

14. Hans Morgenthau, "The Present Tragedy of America," *Worldview,* September 1969.

Chapter 2
INESCAPABLE REALITIES IN A CHANGING WORLD

1. President John F. Kennedy, address on the Nuclear Test Ban Treaty, July 27, 1963.

2. Charles E. Osgood, *An Alternative to War or Surrender* (The University of Illinois Press, 1962), p. 23.

3. Hans J. Morgenthau, *A New Foreign Policy for the United States* (Praeger Publishers, Inc., 1969), p. 240.

4. Robert Heilbroner, interview in *Psychology Today,* February 1975, p. 100.

5. Norman Cousins, editorial in *World,* July 4, 1972, p. 1.

6. Seyom Brown, *New Forces in World Politics* (The Brookings Institution, 1974), p. 138.

7. Mihajlo Mesarovič and Eduard Pestel, *Mankind at the Turning Point* (E. P. Dutton & Co., Inc., 1974), p. 134.

8. James M. Wall, editorial in *The Christian Century,* Oct. 22, 1975, p. 915.

9. Norman Cousins, editorial in *Saturday Review,* Oct. 5, 1974, p. 4.

Chapter 3
EXPERTS, POLICYMAKERS, AND ABSOLUTISTS

1. Richard J. Barnet, *The Roots of War* (Penguin Books, Inc., 1973).

2. Richard J. Barnet and Ronald E. Müller, *Global Reach— The Power of the Multinational Corporation* (Simon & Schuster, Inc., 1974).

3. David Halberstam, *The Best and the Brightest* (Random House, Inc., 1969).

4. Zbigniew Brzezinski, in *Foreign Policy,* Summer 1976, pp. 82–83.

5. Robert F. Kennedy, *Thirteen Days—A Memoir of the*

Cuban Missile Crisis (New American Library, Inc., 1969).

6. Arthur Schlesinger, Jr., *A Thousand Days* (Houghton Mifflin Company, 1965), p. 807.

7. Paul Ramsey, *Who Speaks for the Church?* (Abingdon Press, 1967), pp. 149–153.

8. Townsend Hoopes, *The Limits of Intervention* (David McKay Company, Inc., 1969).

9. *Ibid.,* p. 51.

10. Neil Sheehan, *The Pentagon Papers,* The New York Times edition (Bantam Books, Inc., 1971), p. 234.

11. Max Weber's essay "Politics as a Vocation" has been published in pamphlet form by the Fortress Press, 1965. Also the essay is available in H. H. Gerth and C. Wright Mills, eds., *From Max Weber: Essays in Sociology* (Oxford University Press, 1958).

12. Kennan, "Foreign Policy and Christian Conscience."

SPECIAL NOTE: Secretary Cyrus Vance, when he testified before the Senate committee in connection with his confirmation as Secretary of State, said the following: "In the light of hindsight I believe it was a mistake to have intervened in Vietnam. U.S. involvement was not based on evil motives but on misjudgments and mistakes as we went along." This was an extraordinary repudiation of a most fateful chapter of American foreign policy beginning with our support of the French in Indochina. Five of Vance's predecessors from both parties shared responsiblity for this policy and Vance himself was engaged in implementing it in the Pentagon under President Johnson. It is remarkable that such a confession of so tragic and costly an error did not cause a ripple. It also shows that, while from the point of view of personal character, motives may be most important, when it comes to good judgment about policy, presuppositions and perceptions have decisive importance.

Chapter 4
MORALITY AND NATIONAL INTEREST

1. Article by John Osborn in *The New Republic,* April 10, 1976.

2. Brown, *New Forces in World Politics,* p. 212. See com-

ments in Ch. 6, p. 6, on these statistics concerning American support of the UN in the light of more recent events.

3. Joseph S. Nye, "Independence and Interdependence," *Foreign Policy,* Spring 1976.

4. Article by James W. Fulbright in *The New York Times Magazine,* March 21, 1965.

5. Article by Walter Lippmann in *Newsweek,* April 29, 1963.

Chapter 5
PERSONAL OPTIONS AND MODERN WAR

1. Augustine, *The City of God,* bk. 19, ch. 7 (Marcus Dod's translation).

2. See Roland Bainton, *Christian Attitudes Toward War and Peace* (Abingdon Press, 1960), and Ralph Potter, *War and Moral Discourse* (John Knox Press, 1969).

3. Max Stackhouse, *Ethics of Necropolis* (Beacon Press, Inc., 1971), p. 11.

4. Paul Ramsey, *War and the Christian Conscience* (Duke University Press, 1961), and *The Just War* (Charles Scribner's Sons, 1968).

5. Lester B. Pearson, "Trade, Aid, and Peace," *Saturday Review,* Feb. 22, 1969, p. 26.

6. Second Vatican Council, *Pastoral Constitution on the Church in the Modern World,* par. 80.

7. Hans Morgenthau, "The Nuclear Discussion: Continued," *Christianity and Crisis,* Dec. 11, 1961, p. 223.

8. Pope John XXIII, *Pacem in Terris—Peace on Earth,* par. 127.

9. John C. Bennett, *The Radical Imperative* (The Westminster Press, 1975), pp. 183–184.

10. See Gene Sharp, *The Politics of Nonviolent Action* (Porter Sargent, Publishers, 1973), and Harvey Seifert, *Conquest by Suffering: The Process and Prospects of Nonviolent Resistance* (The Westminster Press, 1965).

Chapter 6
AN EVALUATION OF MILITARY DETERRENCE

1. The Group for the Advancement of Psychiatry, *Psychiatric Aspects of the Prevention of Nuclear War* (Report No. 57, 1964), p. 274.

2. *Ibid.,* p. 238.

3. Fred C. Ikle, "Can Nuclear Deterrence Last Out the Century?" *Foreign Affairs,* January 1973, p. 269. See chs. 5 and 6 of Philip Green, *Deadly Logic: The Theory of Nuclear Deterrence* (Schocken Books, Inc., 1968), for a stimulating discussion of the assumption of rationality in deterrence theory and of the ethical implications of that assumption.

4. Ernest Cuneo, quoted in William O. Douglas, *Anatomy of Liberty* (Simon & Schuster, Inc., 1967), p. 110.

5. Robert W. Gardiner, *The Cool Arm of Destruction* (The Westminster Press, 1974), p. 125.

6. Arthur Simon, *Bread for the World* (Paulist/Newman Press and Wm. B. Eerdmans Publishing Company, 1975), p. 123.

7. Charles Birch, "Creation, Technology and Human Survival," address to the 1975 Nairobi Assembly of the World Council of Churches; Richard J. Barnet, *The Economy of Death* (Atheneum Publishers, 1969), p. 50.

8. William Epstein, "The Disarmament Hoax," *World,* April 10, 1973, pp. 24–25.

9. Barnet, *The Economy of Death,* pp. 5–6.

10. See Seymour Melman, *Our Depleted Society* (Holt, Rinehart & Winston, Inc., 1965) and *The Permanent War Economy* (Simon & Schuster, Inc., 1974).

11. John C. Bennett, *Nuclear Weapons and the Conflict of Conscience* (Charles Scribner's Sons, 1962), p. 109.

12. *Ibid.,* p. 102.

13. *Ibid.,* p. 43.

14. Harrison Brown and James Real in Walter Millis, ed., *A World Without War* (Washington Square Press, Inc., 1961), p. 6.

15. Harlan Cleveland, "The US Versus the UN?" *The New York Times Magazine,* May 4, 1975, p. 19.

16. Morgenthau, *A New Foreign Policy for the United States,* pp. 208, 214.

17. Ramsey Clark, "On Violence, Peace, and the Rule of Law," *Foreign Affairs,* October 1970, p. 233.

18. Jerome Wiesner and Herbert York, "National Security and the Nuclear-Test Ban," *Scientific American,* Oct. 1964, p. 35.

19. Osgood, *An Alternative to War or Surrender.*

20. William Epstein, "Outlook: The Arms Race," *Saturday Review,* June 29, 1974, p. 43.

21. Amitai Etzioni, *Studies in Social Change* (Holt, Rinehart and Winston, Inc., 1966), Ch. 4.

22. Osgood, *An Alternative to War or Surrender,* p. 110.

Chapter 7
POLITICAL STRUCTURES OF INTERDEPENDENCE

1. See Inis L. Claude, Jr., *Power and International Relations* (Random House, Inc., 1962), Ch. 3.

2. See a study of changes in American attitudes toward the UN based upon the Watts-Free surveys in the article "Nationalism, Not Isolationism" in *Foreign Policy,* Fall 1976.

3. Grenville Clark and Louis B. Sohn, *World Peace Through World Law* (Harvard University Press, 1958).

4. Herman Kahn, quoted by Paul Ramsey in *The Limits of Nuclear War* (pamphlet published by Council on Religion and International Affairs, 1963), pp. 26–27.

5. Article by Donald Keyes in *Worldview,* March 1973.

6. Richard Gardiner, "The Hard Road to World Order," *Foreign Affairs,* April 1974, p. 558. The author is now ambassador to Italy.

7. Reinhold Niebuhr, "The Illusion of World Government," article originally published in *Foreign Affairs,* April 1949, also in his *Christian Realism and Political Problems.*

8. Reinhold Niebuhr, an address before the National Conference of UNESCO in New York City, January 1952.

9. Charles W. Yost, *The Conduct and Misconduct of Foreign Affairs* (Random House, Inc., 1972), p. 185.

10. Morgenthau, *Politics Among Nations,* p. 475.

11. Leland M. Goodrich, *The United Nations in a Changing World* (Columbia University Press, 1974), p. 145.

12. Ernest Lefever, *Crisis in the Congo* (The Brookings Institution, 1965), p. 181.

13. Yost, *The Conduct and Misconduct of Foreign Affairs,* p. 132.

14. Goodrich, *The United Nations in a Changing World,* p. 29.

15. Morgenthau, *Politics Among Nations,* p. 474.

16. Nye, "Independence and Interdependence," p. 146.

17. *Ibid.,* p. 147.

Chapter 8
RETHINKING AMERICA'S POLITICAL ROLE IN THE WORLD

1. Manchester *Guardian,* June 27, 1976.
2. Many observers point to this erosion of ideological commitment. Both Hedrick Smith and Robert Kaiser in the books quoted later in this chapter indicate this. Kaiser goes so far as to say the following: "Of the intellectuals I knew, most agreed that a few people still believe passionately in the ideology, but only a few. Some of my acquaintances were certain that no one still believes." (*Russia,* p. 406; Atheneum Publishers, 1976.) In 1966 the American ambassador in Moscow, Foy D. Kohler, said of the Russians that "precisely because they have been exposed to a pernicious and dogmatic ideology, they are in some respects even less ideological than their Western European brothers" (*U.S. News & World Report,* Dec. 26, 1966). The American ambassador in Moscow in 1976, Walter J. Stoessel, said in leaving that office that "ideology is becoming less instrumental in governing Soviet behavior." He added that "in a sense you could say they are perhaps in the process of becoming a more traditional kind of world power." (*The New York Times,* Sept. 12, 1976.)
3. Hedrick Smith, *The Russians* (Quadrangle/The New York Times Book Co., 1976).
4. Kaiser, *Russia.*
5. Smith, *The Russians,* pp. 234–235.
6. Kaiser, *Russia,* p. 463.
7. Hannah Arendt, *On Revolution* (The Viking Press, Inc., Compass Books, 1965), p. 155.
8. Reinhold Niebuhr, *The Children of Light and the Children of Darkness* (Charles Scribner's Sons, 1944).
9. Hans Morgenthau, dialogue with Reinhold Niebuhr, *War/Peace Report,* February 1967.

SPECIAL NOTE: The Carter Administration has shown tendencies or taken actions that begin to correct some of the aspects of American policy criticized in this and in the preceding chapter. It seems to be taking a more positive attitude toward the role of the United Nations. It is moving toward "normalization" of relations between the United States and Vietnam. It has taken steps to establish new relations with Cuba from which we have been so long isolated. It makes much of its avoidance of political intervention in Western Europe to prevent Communist parties from sharing power. It has begun to take a more symmetrical attitude toward violations of human rights by both rightist and leftist governments. The idea seems often implied in public discussion that morality as a factor in foreign policy first appears when human rights are emphasized. This is a strange idea, as concern to prevent war, to control the arms race, to establish many human relations across national boundaries, to promote greater economic and social justice between nations have great moral significance. The survivors of a nuclear war are not likely to have many human rights in any country. It is highly desirable for the United States as a nation to witness consistently to our commitment to the rights of persons so often violated by governments. But consistency needs to be stressed, for our record of strong support for many governments that have been and still are cruel violators of human rights diminishes our credibility. A single-track crusade for individualistic human rights in a world in which so many nations have different histories and priorities from ours may be counterproductive. Most to be emphasized is the example of our government, its quiet pressures where they can do most good, and many kinds of unofficial witness, fact-finding, and action by both national and international groups and agencies.

Chapter 9
INTERNATIONAL ETHICS AND ECONOMIC PRIVILEGE

1. Robert McNamara quoted in *Newsweek,* Sept. 15, 1975, p. 37.
2. Simon, *Bread for the World,* pp. 3–4.
3. James W. Howe *et al., The United States and World Development: Agenda for Action, 1975* (Praeger Publishers, Inc., 1975), pp. 208–109.
4. Simon, *Bread for the World,* p. 45.
5. Robert Lichtman, *Toward Community: A Criticism of Contemporary Capitalism,* an Occasional Paper of the Center for the Study of Democratic Institutions, 1966, p. 17.
6. Barbara Ward and René Dubos, *Only One Earth* (W.W. Norton & Company, Inc., 1972), pp. 24–25.
7. Karl Barth, *Church Dogmatics,* Vol. III, Pt. 4 (Edinburgh: T. & T. Clark, 1961), p. 298.

8. Karl Barth, *Church Dogmatics,* Vol. II, Pt. 1 (Edinburgh: T. & T. Clark, 1957), p. 386.

9. José Míguez-Bonino, *Christians and Marxists* (London: Hodder & Stoughton, Ltd., 1975), p. 40.

10. Gustavo Gutiérrez, *A Theology of Liberation* (Orbis Books, 1973), p. 276.

11. Robert McNamara, *One Hundred Countries, Two Billion People: The Dimensions of Development* (Praeger Publishers, Inc., 1973), p. 9.

12. Ansley J. Coale, "The Economic Effects of Fertility Control in Underdeveloped Areas," in Roy O. Greep, ed., *Human Fertility and Population Problems* (Schenkman Publishing Company, Inc., 1963), p. 159.

13. Edward Fried in Harry Owen, ed., *The Next Phase in Foreign Policy* (The Brookings Institution, 1973), p. 193.

14. Howe *et al., The United States and World Development,* p. 258.

15. Gunnar Myrdal, *The Challenge of World Poverty* (Random House, Inc., Vintage Books, 1971), p. 369. See also pp. 359–363.

16. Paul A. Laudicina, *World Poverty and Development: A Survey of American Opinion* (Overseas Development Council, 1973).

17. U.S. Department of Commerce figures in Howe *et al., The United States and World Development,* p. 259.

Chapter 10
A NEW INTERNATIONAL ECONOMIC ORDER

1. Theodore Hesburgh, Foreword in Howe, *The United States and World Development,* p. vi.

2. Kurt Waldheim, *The Seventh Special Session of the General Assembly* (United Nations pamphlet, 1975), p. 3.

3. Simon, *Bread for the World,* p. 103.

4. Daniel Bell, *The Cultural Contradictions of Capitalism* (Basic Books, Inc., 1976), p. 207.

5. Barnet and Müller, *Global Reach,* p. 26.

6. *Ibid.,* p. 13.

7. Ernest Schumacher, *Small Is Beautiful* (Harper & Row, Publishers, Inc., 1973).

8. Emílio Médici, quoted in Peter Berger, *Pyramids of Sacrifice* (Basic Books, Inc., 1974), p. 148.

9. Chadwick F. Alger, "The Multinational Corporation and

the Future International System," *Annals,* September 1972, pp. 104, 111.

10. Mesarovič and Pestel, *Mankind at the Turning Point,* p. 111.

11. Robert Heilbroner, *Between Capitalism and Socialism* (Random House, Inc., Vintage Books, 1970), p. 53.

12. Alan Geyer, "World Federalism Reconsidered," *Worldview,* November 1974, p. 35.

13. Mesarovič and Pestel, *Mankind at the Turning Point,* p. 54.

14. Ward and Dubos, *Only One Earth,* p. 220.

Chapter 11
RESOURCES OF CHURCHES AND RESISTANCES TO CHANGE

1. Ward and Dubos, *Only One Earth,* p. 212.

2. George W. Ball, *Diplomacy for a Crowded World* (Little, Brown & Company, Atlantic Monthly Book, 1976), pp. 309–312.

3. Barnet, *Roots of War,* p. 316.

4. See Harvey Seifert, *New Power for the Church* (The Westminster Press, 1976), pp. 119–125.

5. Barnet, *Roots of War,* p. 332.

SELECTED BIBLIOGRAPHY

Bainton, Roland, *Christian Attitudes Toward War and Peace.* Abingdon Press, 1960.

Barnet, Richard J., *The Economy of Death.* Atheneum Publishers, 1969.

——*Intervention and Revolution.* World Publishing Co., Inc., 1968.

——*The Roots of War.* Penguin Books, Inc., 1973.

Barnet, Richard J., and Müller, Ronald E., *Global Reach—The Power of the Multinational Corporation.* Simon & Schuster, Inc., 1974.

Bennett, John C., *Christianity and Communism Today.* Association Press, 1970.

——*Foreign Policy in Christian Perspective.* Charles Scribner's Sons, 1966.

—— (ed.), *Nuclear Weapons and the Conflict of Conscience.* Charles Scribner's Sons, 1962.

——*The Radical Imperative.* The Westminster Press, 1975.

Brown, Seyom, *New Forces in World Politics.* The Brookings Institution, 1974.

Butterfield, Herbert, *Christianity, Diplomacy, and War.* Abingdon-Cokesbury Press, 1953.

Claude, Inis L., Jr., *Power and International Relations.* Random House, Inc., 1962.

Finn, James, *Protest: Pacifism and Politics.* Random House, Inc., 1967.

Freudenberger, C. Dean, and Minus, Paul M., Jr., *Christian Responsibility in a Hungry World.* Abingdon Press, 1976.

Gardiner, Robert W., *The Cool Arm of Destruction.* The Westminster Press, 1974.

Goodrich, Leland, *The United Nations in a Changing World.* Columbia University Press, 1974.

Heilbroner, Robert, *Between Capitalism and Socialism.* Random House, Inc., Vintage Books, 1970.

———*The Great Ascent.* Harper & Row, Publishers, Inc., 1963.

———*An Inquiry Into the Human Prospect.* W.W. Norton & Company, Inc., 1974.

Hoffman, Stanley H., ed., *Contemporary Theory in International Relations.* Prentice-Hall, Inc., 1960.

Howe, James W., *et al., The United States and World Development: Agenda for Action, 1975.* Praeger Publishers, Inc., 1975.

Kahn, Herman, *On Escalation—Metaphors and Scenarios.* Praeger Publishers, Inc., 1965.

Kennedy, Robert F., *Thirteen Days—A Memoir of the Cuban Missile Crisis.* New American Library, Inc., 1969.

Kolko, Joyce, and Kolko, Gabriel, *The Limits of Power.* Harper & Row, Publishers, Inc., 1972.

Long, Edward L., Jr., *War and Conscience in America.* The Westminster Press, 1968.

Medvedev, Roy A., *Let History Judge.* Alfred A. Knopf, Inc., 1976.

Melman, Seymour, *Pentagon Capitalism: The Political Economy of War.* McGraw-Hill Book Co., Inc., 1970.

———*The Permanent War Economy.* Simon & Schuster, Inc., 1974.

Morgenthau, Hans J., *A New Foreign Policy for the United States.* Praeger Publishers, Inc., 1969.

———*Politics Among Nations.* 5th ed. Alfred A. Knopf, Inc., 1974.

Myrdal, Gunnar, *The Challenge of World Poverty.* Random House, Inc., Vintage Books, 1971.

Niebuhr, Reinhold, *Christian Realism and Political Problems.* Charles Scribner's Sons, 1953.

———*Moral Man and Immoral Society.* Charles Scribner's Sons, 1932.

———*The Structure of Nations and Empires.* Charles Scribner's Sons, 1959.

Osgood, Charles E., *An Alternative to War or Surrender.* The University of Illinois Press, 1962.

Potter, Ralph, *War and Moral Discourse.* John Knox Press, 1969.

Ramsey, Paul, *The Just War.* Charles Scribner's Sons, 1968.

———*War and the Christian Conscience.* Duke University Press, 1961.

Seifert, Harvey, *Conquest by Suffering: The Process and Prospects of Nonviolent Resistance.* The Westminster Press, 1965.

——*Ethical Resources for International Relations.* The Westminster Press, 1964.

——*Ethical Resources for Political and Economic Decision.* The Westminster Press, 1972.

Sharp, Gene, *The Politics of Nonviolent Action.* Porter Sargent, Publishers, 1973.

Simon, Arthur, *Bread for the World.* Paulist/Newman Press and Wm. B. Erdmans Publishing Company, 1975.

Stone, Ronald H., *Reinhold Niebuhr—Prophet to Politicians.* Abingdon Press, 1972.

Swomley, John, *American Empire: The Political Ethics of Twentieth Century Conquest.* The Macmillan Company, 1970.

——*Liberation Ethics.* The Macmillan Company, 1972.

Tucker, Robert W., *The Just War.* The Johns Hopkins Press, 1960.

Ward, Barbara, and Dubos, René, *Only One Earth.* W.W. Norton & Company, Inc., 1972.

Yost, Charles W., *The Conduct and Misconduct of Foreign Affairs.* Random House, Inc., 1972.